WINGS

Harcourt Brace & Company

SIGNATURES

WINGS

Senior Authors

Roger C. Farr

Dorothy S. Strickland

Authors

Richard F. Abrahamson ◆ Alma Flor Ada ◆ Barbara Bowen Coulter

Bernice E. Cullinan ◆ Margaret A. Gallego

W. Dorsey Hammond

Nancy Roser ◆ Junko Yokota ◆ Hallie Kay Yopp

Senior Consultant

Asa G. Hilliard III

Consultants

V. Kanani Choy ◆ Lee Bennett Hopkins ◆ Stephen Krashen ◆ Rosalia Salinas

Harcourt Brace & Company

Orlando Atlanta Austin Boston San Francisco Chicago Dallas New York Toronto London

All rights reserved. No part of this publication may be reproduced or transmitted in any form or by any means, electronic or mechanical, including photocopy, recording, or any information storage and retrieval system, without permission in writing from the publisher.

Requests for permission to make copies of any part of the work should be mailed to: Permissions Department, Harcourt Brace & Company, 6277 Sea Harbor Drive, Orlando, Florida 32887-6777.

HARCOURT BRACE and Quill Design is a registered trademark of Harcourt Brace & Company.

Acknowledgments appear in the back of this work.

Printed in the United States of America

ISBN 0-15-306401-3

7 8 9 10   048   99 98

Dear Reader,

The boy on the cover of this book is soaring on the wings of his imagination. You, too, are invited to let your imagination fly free. The selections in **Wings** will let you explore new ideas and places. You will find out how people use their creativity, how they discover their courage, and how teamwork can make a job more fun.

Maybe **Wings** will challenge you to put your own creativity to work or to discover your own courage. Some stories in **Wings** may make you want to be a part of a team. Others will help you learn about cultures in different parts of the United States and of the world.

Remember, your imagination is your pair of wings. With imagination, each story, poem, and article you read can become the ticket to an imaginary journey.

We hope you enjoy the literature in **Wings**. Let your imagination fly free!

Sincerely,

The Authors

The Authors

FAMILIES
POEMS CELEBRATING THE AFRICAN AMERICAN EXPERIENCE

Selected by Dorothy S. Strickland
and Michael R. Strickland
Illustrations by John Ward

ISLA

BY ARTHUR DORROS
illustrated by ELISA KLEVEN

National Geographic
World

BONUS
SUPERFUN
INSIDE

**Appelemando's
Dreams**
PATRICIA POLACCO

6

CREATIVITY AT WORK

CONTENTS

13 Theme Opener

16 Bookshelf

Fantasy/Social Studies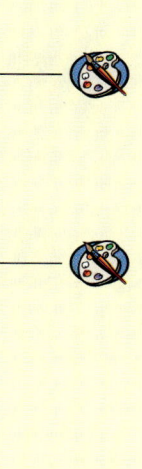

18 Isla
*by Arthur Dorros
illustrated by Elisa Kleven*

**Profile: Arthur Dorros
and Elisa Kleven**

Expository Nonfiction/Science

42 Sleeping and Dreaming
by Rita Milios

Art

58 Art and Literature:
*Pa'ndau
Hmong Story Cloth*

Fantasy/Social Studies

60 Appelemando's Dreams
*written and illustrated by
Patricia Polacco*

Profile: Patricia Polacco

Expository Nonfiction/Science

88 What Is Color?
by Neil Ardley

Magazine Article/Art

94 Zeny's Zoo
from *National Geographic
World* magazine

Biography/Art

96 Jerry Pinkney:
Achiever of Dreams
by Ilene Cooper

Profile: Ilene Cooper

Poem

104 Parent to Child
by Naomi F. Faust

108 Theme Wrap-Up

DISCOVERING COURAGE

CONTENTS

109 **Theme Opener**

112 **Bookshelf**

Fiction/Science

114 **Brave Irene**
*written and illustrated by
William Steig*

    Profile: William Steig

Realistic Fiction/Science

134 **Storm in the Night**
*by Mary Stolz
illustrated by Pat Cummings*

    Profile: Pat Cummings

Play/Science

162 **The Mystery of
the Sounds in the Night**
by Joan Lowery Nixon

Poem

172 **A wolf . . .**
Teton Sioux Song

Poem

174 **When I Wake**
*by Jonathan London
illustrated by David Diaz*

Art

176 **Art and Literature:**
*The Diving Board
by Norman Rockwell*

Realistic Fiction/Social Studies

178 **Lester's Dog**
*by Karen Hesse
illustrated by Nancy Carpenter*

    **Profile: Karen Hesse and
Nancy Carpenter**

Magazine Article/Health

210 **Think Positive!**
from *Current Health 1* magazine

Realistic Fiction/Social Studies

216 **My Name Is
María Isabel**
by Alma Flor Ada

    Profile: Alma Flor Ada

Poem

232 **How a Girl Got Her
Chinese Name**
by Nellie Wong

236 **Theme
Wrap-Up**

10

CONTENTS ᴛʜᴇ POWER ᴏғ TEAMWORK

237 Theme Opener

240 Bookshelf

Realistic Fiction/Social Studies

242 City Green
written and illustrated by
DyAnne DiSalvo-Ryan

Profile: DyAnne DiSalvo-Ryan

Magazine Article/Physical Education

258 Kids and Kicks
by Deborah H. DeFord
from *U.S. Kids* magazine

Poem

262 The New Kid
by Mike Makley

Realistic Fiction/Physical Education

264 Centerfield Ballhawk
by Matt Christopher

Profile: Matt Christopher

Poems

276 Playing Outfield *and*
Prediction: School P.E.
by Isabel Joshlin Glaser

Russian Folktale

280 The Turnip
retold by Pleasant DeSpain

Poem

284 After the Last
Hard Freeze
by Arnold Adoff
illustrated by Jerry Pinkney

Art

286 Art and Literature:
Detroit Industry
by Diego Rivera

Chinese Folktale/Social Studies

288 Lon Po Po: A Red-Riding
Hood Story from China
translated and illustrated by
Ed Young

Profile: Ed Young

Southwestern Folktale/Social Studies

312 The Three Little
Javelinas
by Susan Lowell
illustrated by Jim Harris

Profile: Susan Lowell
and Jim Harris

332 Theme Wrap-Up

333 Glossary

346 Index of Titles
and Authors

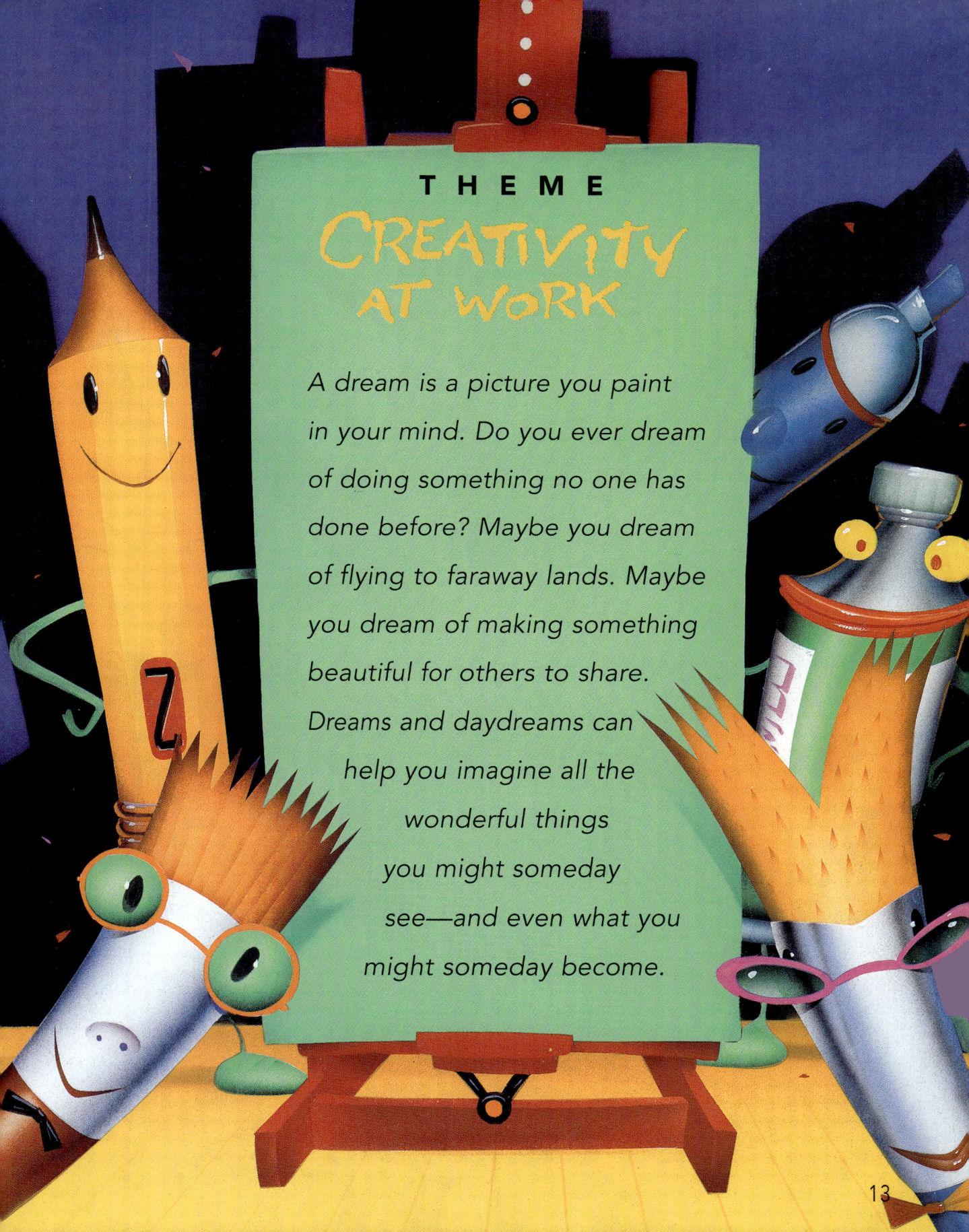

T H E M E

CREATIVITY AT WORK

A dream is a picture you paint in your mind. Do you ever dream of doing something no one has done before? Maybe you dream of flying to faraway lands. Maybe you dream of making something beautiful for others to share. Dreams and daydreams can help you imagine all the wonderful things you might someday see—and even what you might someday become.

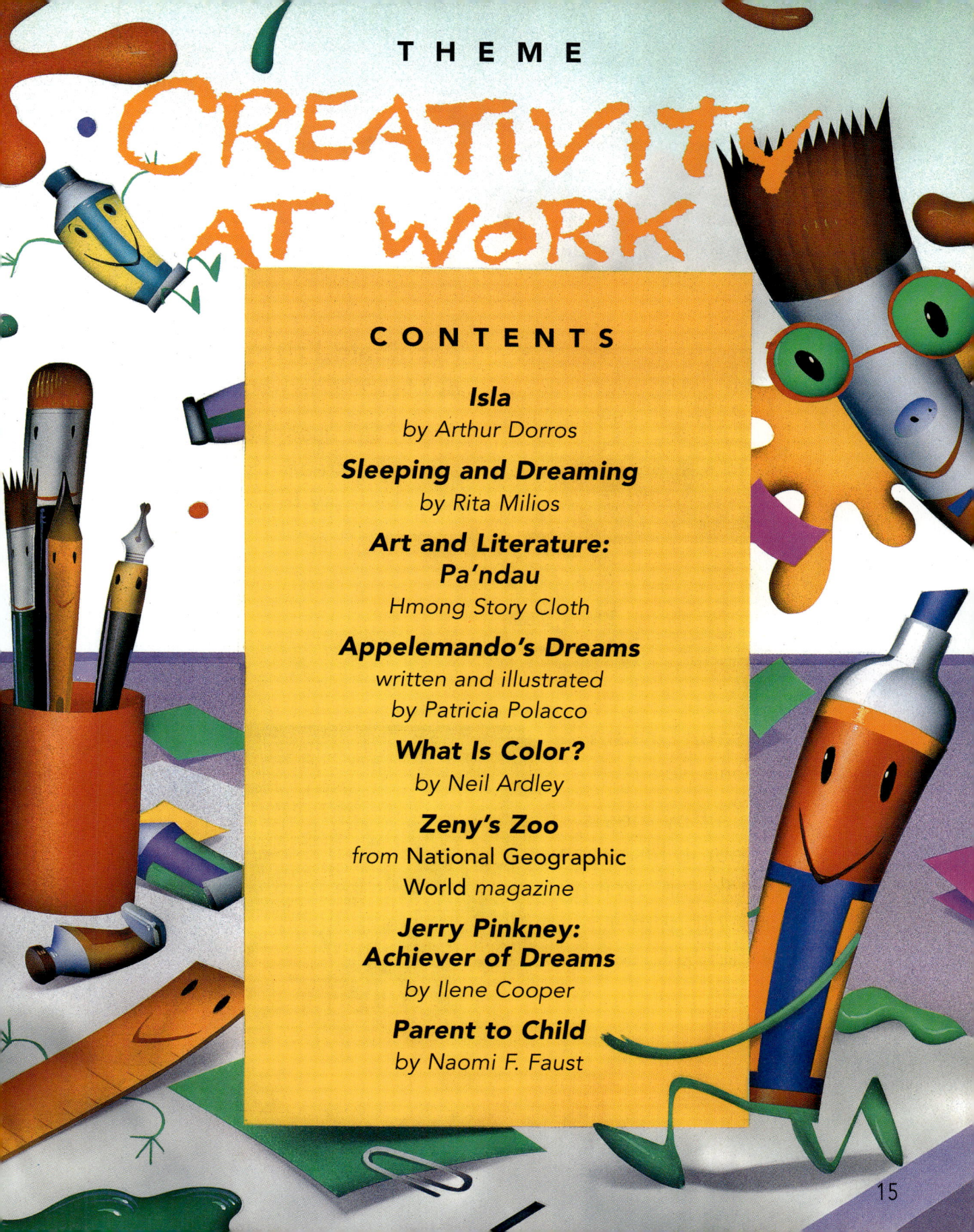

CREATIVITY AT WORK

CONTENTS

Isla
by Arthur Dorros

Sleeping and Dreaming
by Rita Milios

Art and Literature: Pa'ndau
Hmong Story Cloth

Appelemando's Dreams
written and illustrated by Patricia Polacco

What Is Color?
by Neil Ardley

Zeny's Zoo
from National Geographic World magazine

Jerry Pinkney: Achiever of Dreams
by Ilene Cooper

Parent to Child
by Naomi F. Faust

BOOKSHELF

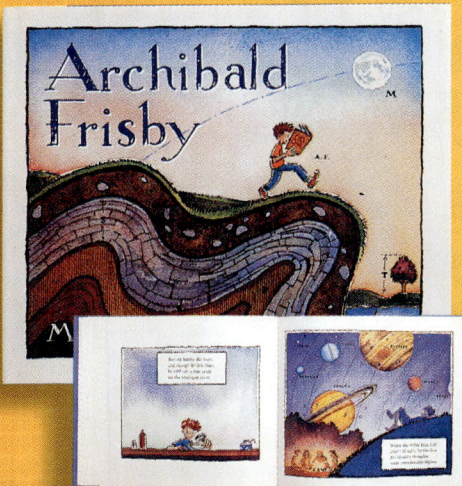

Archibald Frisby
by Michael Chesworth

Archibald uses his scientific creativity to help his new friends at camp.

Signatures Library

Dinosaur Dream
by Dennis Nolan

When a boy meets a dinosaur in his dream, they take an exciting journey together.

Award-Winning Author and Illustrator

Signatures Library

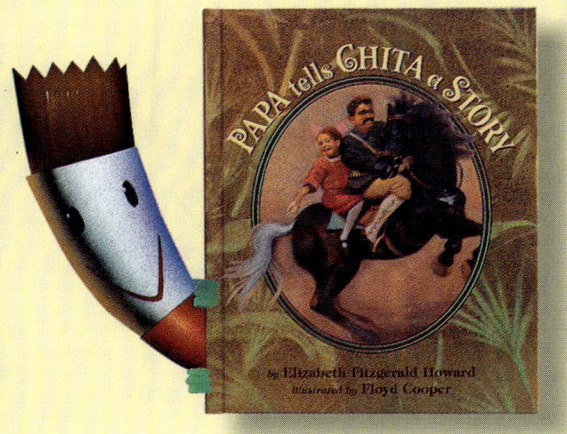

Papa Tells Chita a Story
by Elizabeth Fitzgerald Howard

Chita loves to hear—and add to—her father's stories about the Spanish-American War in Cuba.
Award-Winning Illustrator

The Color of Things
by Vivienne Shalom

Jill and her friends save their town from a future without color.

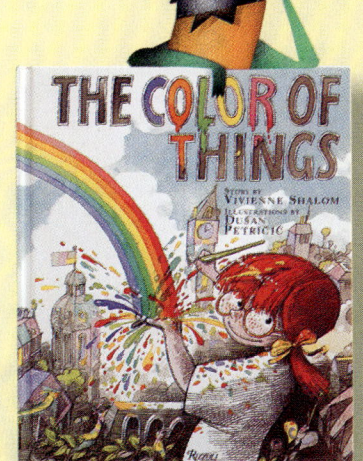

The Piñata Maker/ *El Piñatero*
by George Ancona

In English and Spanish, this book tells the true story of a Mexican artist who makes special piñatas.
Notable Trade Book in Social Studies

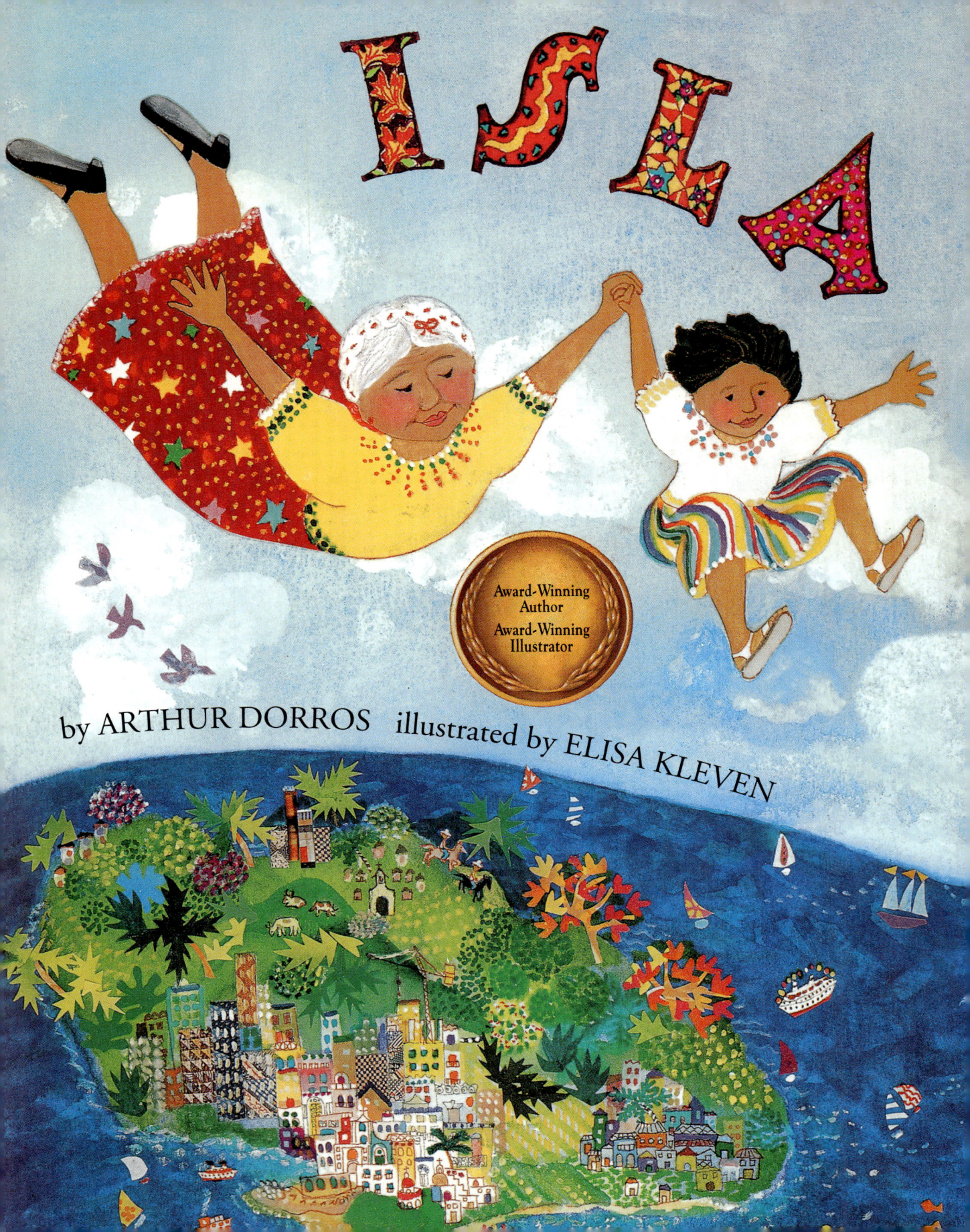

ISLA

by ARTHUR DORROS   illustrated by ELISA KLEVEN

When Abuela, my grandma, tells me stories, we can fly anywhere. Today she's telling me about *la isla,* the island where she grew up. We are flying there together.

We travel a long, long way to where it is always warm.

"¡Mira!" Abuela calls. *"Mi esmeralda."*

I look. I see her island sparkling like a green jewel in the sea.

"Aire tropical," says Abuela, taking a deep breath. The hot, damp air smells salty.

We fly over forests, fields, and tiny towns to visit *tío* Fernando, *tía* Isabel, and my cousin Elena. Even though we're up high, they see us and wave.

Tío Fernando is my uncle, my *mamá's* brother.
Abuela is their mother.
She raised them on *la isla.*

"*¡Bienvenidas!*" *Tío* Fernando welcomes us. He and my
mamá grew up in this house with Abuela and Abuelo,
my grandfather. Abuelo died before I was born. Now *tío*
Fernando lives here with his family. I think he looks like my
mamá, except he has a beard.

"*El osito,*" Abuela calls him—the little bear.

Abuela shows me all around.

In the front room, she and Abuelo used to run a little store.

On the wall, next to a picture of the store, is a painting of *tío* Fernando with a giant fish.

"¡Qué pescado!" Abuela says, telling me what a fish it was.

Tío Fernando found it in a shallow stream.

He brought it home to keep for a pet.

Abuela said the fish would be happier in the river.

Tío Fernando was sad to see it go, so Abuela painted the picture for him.

"Los niños," Abuela says, showing me a picture of some children.

It's my *mamá* and *tío* Fernando playing in a fountain.

Abuela and Abuelo built the fountain with stones from the rain forest.

It is still in the yard.

"Es mágica," Abuela says.

The fountain does seem magical.

The water splashing over stones sounds like birds singing.

Now Abuela wants to show me more of *la isla.*

Elena says she'll meet us later at the beach.

"¡Que disfruten!" she calls. She wants us to have fun.

"*Vamos a la selva,*" says Abuela.
We're going to the rain forest where the fountain
stones came from.
We fly there with parrots flapping beside us.
The treetops are a bright garden, I tell Abuela.
"*Y una sombrilla,*" Abuela says.
They are an umbrella, too.

Down below, it is dark and cool.
"*Como la noche,*" like night, Abuela tells me.
But she can scoop up a tree frog or a lizard
running on a leaf.

Forest eyes are open wide.
My eyes are open, too.
"*Hay mucho más que ver,*" Abuela says, taking off.
There is much more for us to see.

We fly to the busy old city, zooming between colored buildings and over blue brick streets.

Above the square, Abuela and I spin and dip for the people below. *"Pájaros grandes jugando,"* Abuela says, and laughs. We are like big birds playing.

We zoom down to the harbor, where the big ships are. *"De todo el mundo,"* Abuela tells me. They come from all over the world.

"¡Mira!" She points to a large building. It was made by Spanish people who sailed to the island hundreds of years ago.

Abuela and Abuelo used to come to the city
to buy things for their store.
"Ha cambiado," Abuela sighs. The city has
changed.
Now there are tall buildings and parking lots
and supermarkets.
"Vamos al viejo mercado," she says.
She wants to go to an old market.
And we do go, soaring above highways . . .

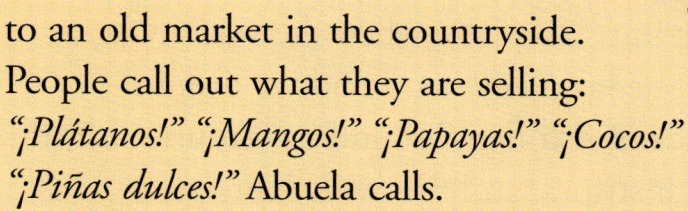

to an old market in the countryside.
People call out what they are selling:
"¡Plátanos!" "¡Mangos!" "¡Papayas!" "¡Cocos!"
"¡Piñas dulces!" Abuela calls.

When she was little, her family grew sweet
pineapples to bring to the market.
The market is hot and crowded.
Soon we are ready to cool off.

"*Vamos a nadar,*" Abuela says.
She used to swim here when she was my age.
"*Ven.*" She takes my hand and we dive in.
All kinds of fish flash around us—round fish, thin fish,
fish with stripes, and fish with spots.

Abuela leaps and dives, too.
"*Nuestro circo,*" she says.
We have our own circus.
"*Mi pez volador.*" She tells me I'm her flying fish.

Tía Isabel, *tío* Fernando, and cousin Elena join us.
Tío Fernando is wearing his snorkeling goggles.
Abuela jokes that he looks like a forest frog.
We float on our backs, and the water meets the sky.
We can float anywhere.

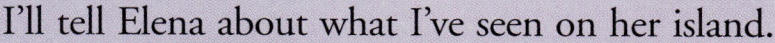

When we get home, we're hungry from our swimming.
"Volemos," Abuela calls.
We fly up into the treetop to pick ripe mangos.
Our hands get sticky from the syrupy juice.
Abuela picks the ripest ones for Elena and me.
We'll help make a salad with mangos and other island fruits.
I'll tell Elena about what I've seen on her island.

After our meal, we sit out in the garden.
Birds, insects, even frogs are chirping.
"Nos cantan." Abuela says they are singing to us.
The plants around us smell sweet and strong.
It feels like the garden is our room, with *las estrellas,*
the stars, our ceiling.
"Ya es hora de partir," Abuela announces.
It is time to go.
The stars will light our way.

We fly through the night, back, back, toward home.
When we see New York City,
the lights look like thousands of stars.

"Es mágica," I say to Abuela.
"Sí," she agrees. *"Es mágica."*

33

After so much flying, we need to sleep.
Abuela asks me what I'm thinking about.
"La isla," I tell her.
"Nuestra isla," she tells me.
I do feel like it is our island.
We can visit it anytime.
"Pronto," Abuela says.
Soon.

35

GLOSSARY

The capitalized syllable is stressed in pronunciation.

Abuela (ah-BWEH-lah) Grandmother

Abuelo (ah-BWEH-loh) Grandfather

Aire tropical (EYE-reh troh-pee-KAHL) Tropical air

Bienvenidas (byehn-veh-NEE-dahs) Welcome

Cocos (COH-cohs) Coconuts

Como la noche (COH-moh lah NOH-cheh) Like the night

De todo el mundo (deh TOH-doh ehl MOON-doh) From all the world

El osito (ehl oh-SEE-toh) The little bear

Es mágica (ehs MAH-hee-kah) It's magic

Ha cambiado (ah cahm-bee-YAH-doh) It has changed

Hay mucho más que ver (eye MOO-cho mahs kay behr) There is much more to see

La isla (lah EES-lah) The island

Las estrellas (lahs ehs-TREH-yahs) The stars

Los niños (lohs NEE-nyohs) The children

Mamá (mah-MAH) Mama

Mangos (MAHN-gohs) Mangos

Mi esmeralda (mee ehs-meh-RAHL-dah) My emerald

Mi pez volador (mee pehs voh-lah-DOHR) My flying fish

Mira (MEE-rah) Look

Nos cantan (nohs CAHN-tahn) They sing to us

Nuestra isla (NWEHS-trah EES-lah) Our island

Nuestro circo (NWEHS-troh SEER-coh) Our circus

Ojos abiertos (OH-hohs ah-BYEHR-tohs) Eyes open

Pájaros grandes jugando (PAH-hah-rohs GRAHN-dehs hoo-GAHN-doh) Big birds playing

Papayas (pah-PIE-yahs) Papayas

Piñas dulces (PEE-nyahs DOOL-sehs) Sweet pineapples

Plátanos (PLAH-tah-nohs) Plantains

Pronto (PROHN-toh) Soon

Que disfruten (kay dees-FROO-tehn) Enjoy

Qué pescado (kay pehs-KAH-doh) What a fish

Sí (see) Yes

Tía (TEE-ah) Aunt

Tío (TEE-oh) Uncle

Vamos a la selva (BAH-mohs ah lah SELL-vah) Let's go to the forest

Vamos al viejo mercado (Bah-mohs ahl bee-YEH-hoh mehr-CAH-doh) Let's go to an old market

Vamos a nadar (BAH-mohs ah nah-DAHR) Let's go swimming

Ven (behn) Come

Volemos (boh-LEH-mohs) Let's fly

Ya es hora de partir (yah ehs OH-rah deh pahr-TEER) Now it is time to leave

Y una sombrilla (ee OO-nah sohm-BREE-yah) And an umbrella

Meet Arthur Dorros

Dear Reader,

When I was a child, I wanted to be able to fly like a bird. I loved to be up high, and I spent a lot of days climbing trees. I still love the idea of flying. When I lived in New York City, the roof of my apartment building was my favorite place.

I spent a lot of time with my grandmother when I was young. We were very close. My grandmother was very adventurous and had many stories to tell about her travels. I loved to listen to her stories and share her adventures.

In "Isla," the little girl's *abuela* is like my own grandmother in many ways. My grandmother lived in Europe until her family moved to the United States. The grandmother in "Isla" moved to the United States from Latin America.

People come to America from many different places. The stories they tell can help us understand other parts of the world. This way, we too can imagine we are flying over places like "Isla."

Sincerely,

Arthur Dorros

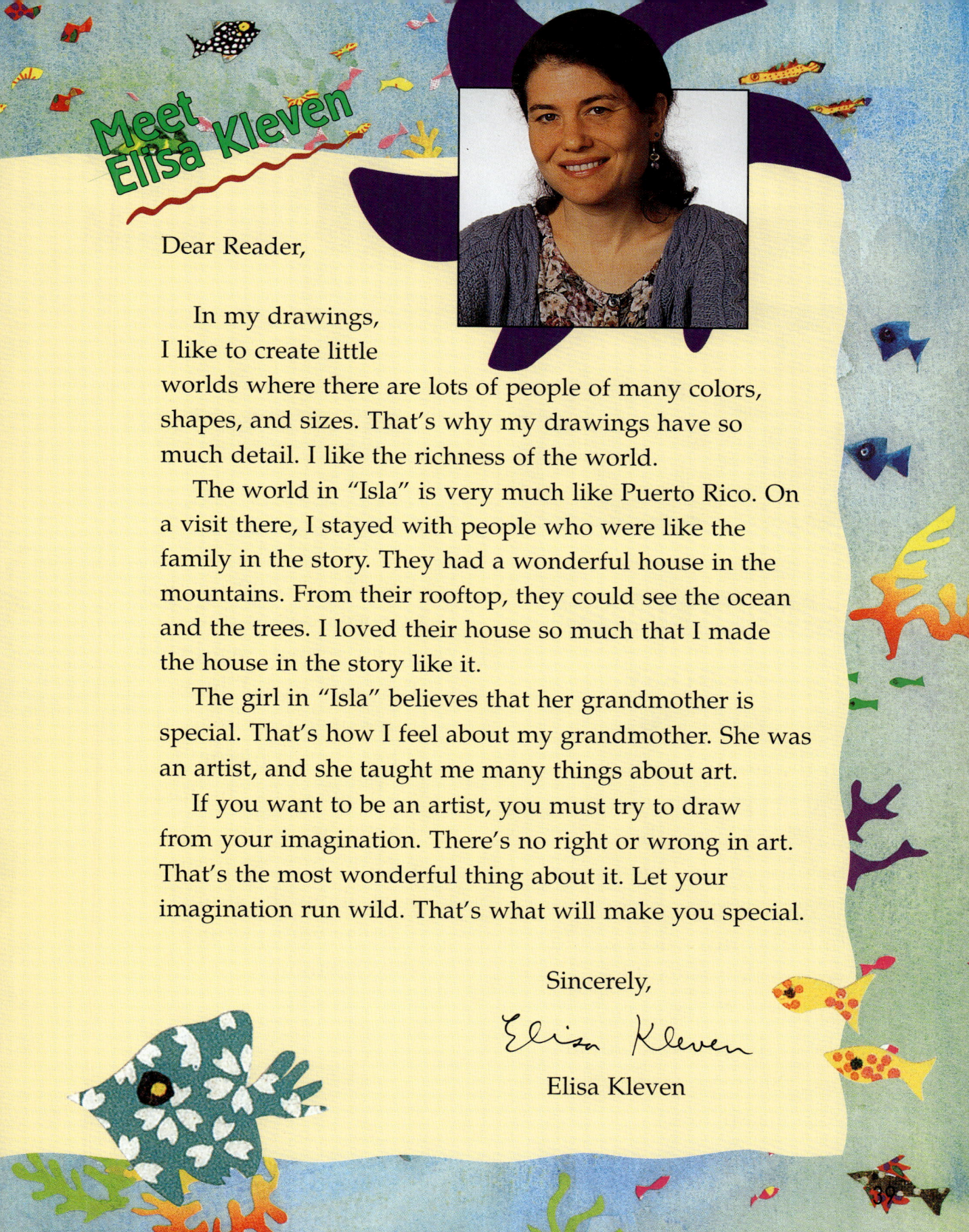

Meet Elisa Kleven

Dear Reader,

In my drawings, I like to create little worlds where there are lots of people of many colors, shapes, and sizes. That's why my drawings have so much detail. I like the richness of the world.

The world in "Isla" is very much like Puerto Rico. On a visit there, I stayed with people who were like the family in the story. They had a wonderful house in the mountains. From their rooftop, they could see the ocean and the trees. I loved their house so much that I made the house in the story like it.

The girl in "Isla" believes that her grandmother is special. That's how I feel about my grandmother. She was an artist, and she taught me many things about art.

If you want to be an artist, you must try to draw from your imagination. There's no right or wrong in art. That's the most wonderful thing about it. Let your imagination run wild. That's what will make you special.

Sincerely,

Elisa Kleven

Elisa Kleven

RESPONSE

WRITE A STORY

Fantasy Vacation

In the story, the young girl and her grandmother can travel anywhere they want by using their imagination. If you could go anywhere in the world, where would you go? Why would you go there? Write a story about the trip you would take. Share your story with your classmates.

DRAW PICTURES

At Home in the Rain Forest

Use an encyclopedia or a science book to find out about animals that live in the rain forest. Choose three or four animals. Then draw a picture of each one in its rain forest home. At the bottom of each picture, write some facts about the animal. Display your pictures in the classroom.

CORNER

WRITE A PARAGRAPH

Two Homes

The grandmother in the story lives in New York now, but she used to live on *la isla*. The two places are very different. Write a paragraph telling how the island is like a big city and how it is different.

What Do You Think?

- Why did the grandmother in the story want to "fly" to the island where she grew up?

- What stories have your family members told you about where they grew up? Would you want to go there?

- How do you think the young girl felt about meeting family members for the first time?

41

Sleeping and

Dreaming

by Rita Milios

Why Do We Sleep?

We all need sleep. Sleep rests our bodies. It allows time for our brains to do certain jobs, such as the making of memory records.

Some people seem to need more sleep than others do. Some healthy adults get by on six hours of sleep with no ill effects. Others feel tired if they sleep less than ten to twelve hours per night.

Babies sleep about eighteen hours a day.

Babies sleep about eighteen hours a day. But by the time most people are ten years old, they have cut their sleep time to nine or ten hours per night. During their teenage years, most people have another drop in sleep time. A "normal" night's sleep for a teenager is about eight hours a night.

Every night when you go to sleep, you enter a strange and wonderful world—the world of your sleep and dreams.

What Happens When We Sleep?

Even though you are not aware of it, your mind does not "turn off" when you sleep. Your brain continues to be active.

Scientists have recorded the sleep of adults. They have found that there is a pattern to this brain activity. This pattern or cycle repeats itself about every one and one-half hours, or about four to six times per night.

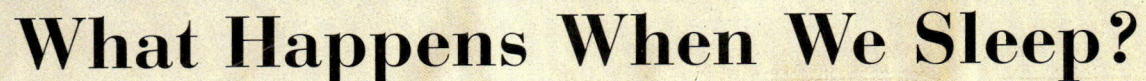

Sleep rests our bodies.

47

All night long, you are moving back and forth from a deeper sleep to a lighter sleep. You spend the most time in your deepest sleep stage during your first sleep cycle of the night. But as the cycles progress, you spend less and less time in deep sleep. During the last sleep cycle of the night, you spend most of your time in light sleep.

There are two main types of sleep, REM and NON-REM. Your REM (rapid eye movement) sleep is a lighter sleep when your dreams occur. During NON-REM sleep your body rests and re-energizes itself. People do not remember the events that occur during NON-REM sleep.

During REM sleep, your light sleep cycle, a strange thing occurs. Many physical changes take place in your body. Your pulse[1] and

---

[1]pulse: the beating of your arteries, caused by your heartbeat

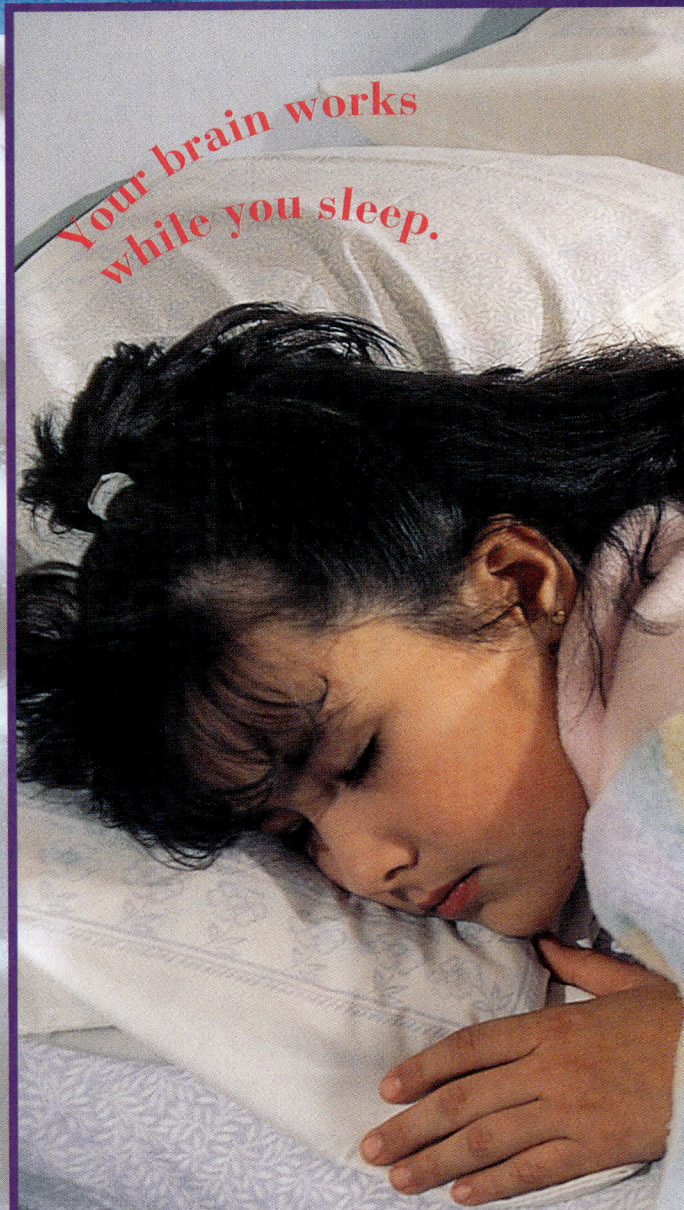

Your brain works while you sleep.

Graphs record brain wave activity during different periods of sleep.

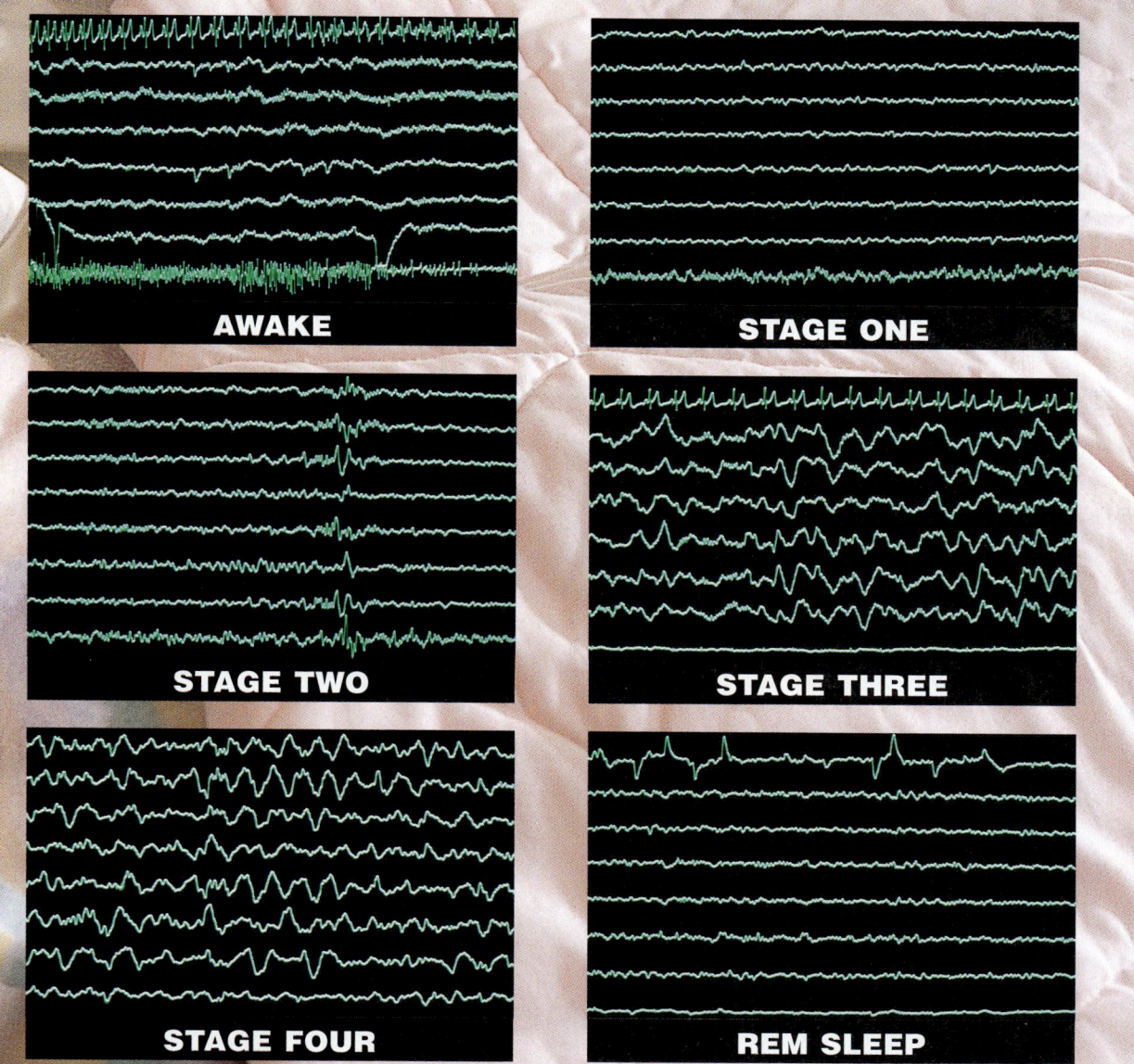

AWAKE

STAGE ONE

STAGE TWO

STAGE THREE

STAGE FOUR

REM SLEEP

respiration[2] may suddenly rise and fall. Your eyes move in short, rapid, jerky movements. (For this reason, this sleep is called rapid eye movement, or REM, sleep.)

[2]respiration: breathing

It is in the periods of REM sleep that your dreams occur. Since much of your final sleep time is REM sleep, you may wake up and remember a dream.

Why Do We Dream?

Some people think that they do not dream. But scientists tell us that we all have dreams during our REM sleep. Some people just don't remember their dreams.

Remembering a dream can be helpful. Sometimes in a dream we recall things we may have forgotten during the day. Dreams help our brains "process" the day's information.

NOT ALL SLEEPING IS DONE AT NIGHT OR IN BED.

Older people do not need as much sleep.

Teenagers sleep about eight hours.

Other times, dreams give us messages about ourselves. These messages come from our "inner selves," often called our subconscious mind. It is called subconscious because it works below the level of our conscious, or waking, awareness. Your subconscious mind uses your dreams to give you information and ideas you may not have noticed during the day.

Creative Dreams

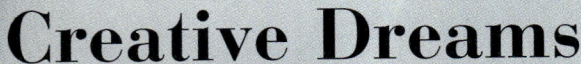

People who create things—writers, musicians, scientists, inventors, or artists—often have ideas "pop" into their minds. Sometimes these thoughts come to people while they are awake. These ideas are called intuitions or inspirations. Other times they come in a dream—a creative dream.

The famous composer Wolfgang Mozart told people that his music came to him in dreams. He created his masterpieces by simply writing down the notes to the music he heard in his dreams.

Mozart wrote operas and symphonies. He said his music came to him in his dreams.

You can have creative dreams, too. Try thinking about a plan, project, or problem just before you go to sleep. You may find that when you "sleep on it," an idea will come to you in a dream.

Odd Sleep Habits and Myths About Sleeping

Some people think they are awake when they are actually still sleeping. Sleepwalking is sometimes called somnambulism. It is more likely to happen to young children, but it does happen to adults, too.

Sleepwalkers can walk about the house and around furniture unhurt. Their subconscious mind "sees," but their conscious (waking) mind does not remember what happens.

Sleepwalkers sometimes do funny things. Once a lady in England awoke to find that her sleepwalking butler had set a table for fourteen upon her bed!

Benjamin Franklin had some odd ideas about sleep.

Some people had strange beliefs about sleep. Benjamin Franklin felt that cool skin was important to a good night's sleep. He slept with the windows open, even in freezing weather. He even suggested everybody should have two beds. When one bed got warm, the person could move to the cool bed!

Thomas Edison thought that sleep was a waste of time and a mark of stupidity. He claimed he slept only about two hours a night. In fact, he slept about four hours per night. He also took many short naps during the day. Today we know that the time he spent during these naps was a time of great creativity. Perhaps we owe the light bulb to one of Edison's catnaps!

RESPONSE

A Zzzzzzz Log

Keep a log, or record, of your sleep for one week. In your log, tell the time you go to bed and the time you wake up. Also, tell whether or not you feel tired the next day. At the end of the week, read your log. Are you getting enough sleep to keep you feeling your best?

What Happens First?

Dreams can sometimes help you solve problems in your life. They might help you figure out where to look for something you lost. They might give you ideas about how to get along with a classmate or a teacher. Draw a cartoon that shows what happens in one dream. Show how a problem is solved in the dream.

CORNER

WRITE A POEM

Sweet Dreams

Think about a dream that made you happy. Maybe you dreamed that you became an actor or took part in the Olympics. Maybe you found money or flew like a bird. Write a poem about your wonderful dream.

What Do You Think?

▶ Why is it important to get enough sleep?

▶ How can dreams help you?

▶ What else would you like to know about sleeping and dreaming? How might you find out these things?

ART & LITERATURE

*S*ome people, like Abuela, tell stories with words. Other people sew stories onto cloth. This story cloth tells about people who left their home to find a better place to live. How can your imagination help you understand how the people in the story cloth feel?

Pa'ndau (1981)
Hmong Story Cloth

A Hmong story cloth is made with a type of artwork called pa'ndau (pän•dou). This is part of a cloth that shows Hmong people leaving their mountain home in China. Some of them are traveling to Laos, Vietnam, and Burma. Later, many Hmong people went to Thailand.

59

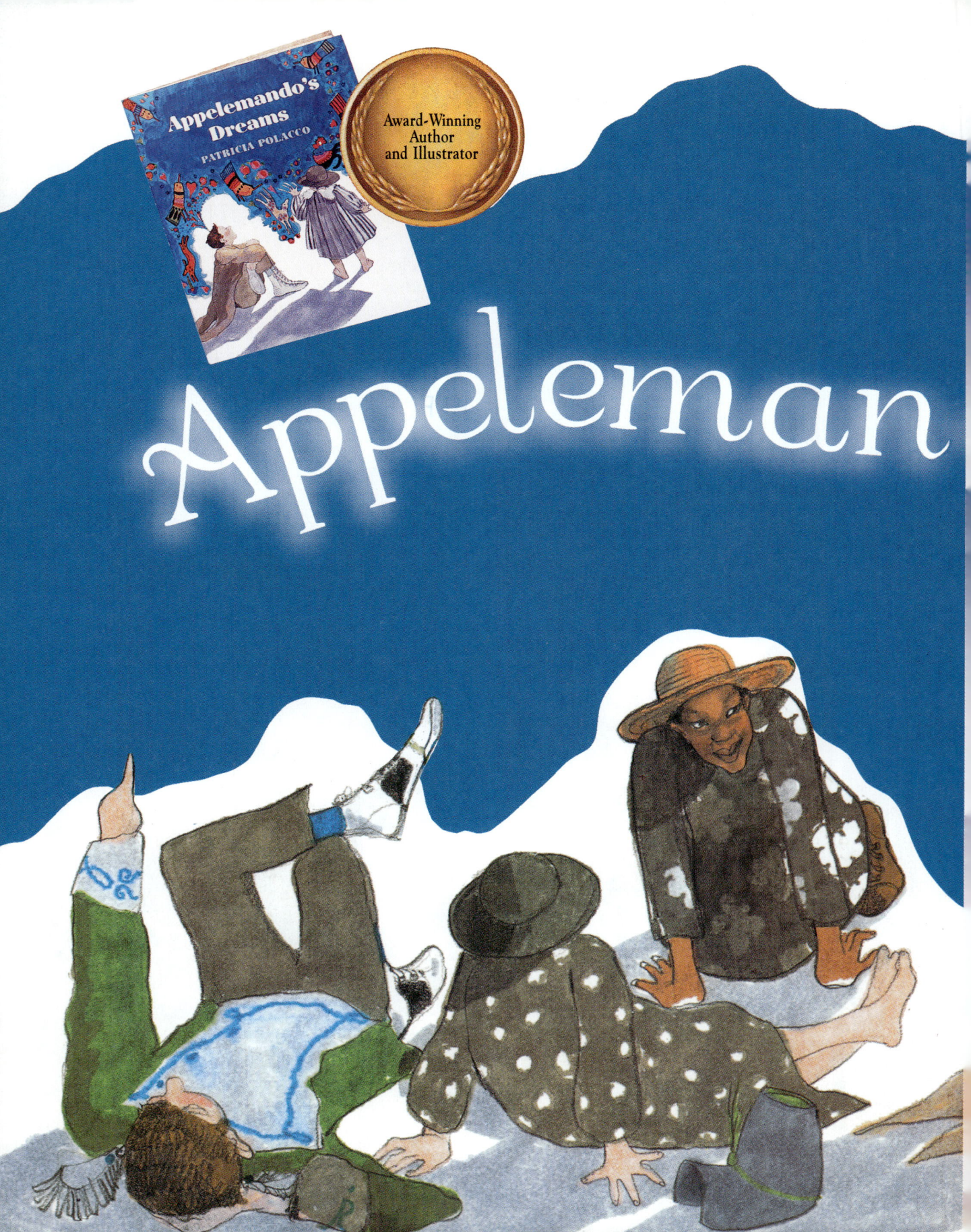

Appelemando's
Dreams

PATRICIA POLACCO

Award-Winning
Author
and Illustrator

Appeleman

do's Dreams

PATRICIA POLACCO

Once there was a very drab village, so drab, in fact, that the road leading to it was overgrown from lack of visitors and interest. There wasn't much to do there. Especially for a little boy named Appelemando. A boy who loved to dream.

For him, dreams were magic chariots pulled through his mind by galloping hues of color. For him, dreaming was a way of life. He dreamt so much of the time that the villagers began to talk.

"There goes that slow Appelemando," they called after him.

"He'll never amount to much."

"He never does anything useful."

"He dreams the day away."

Appelemando had four good and true friends.
"Don't listen to them," Jefftoe Fury said quietly.
"What do they know?" Lark Apostanoff snapped.
Petra and Dorma Opatoshoe cooed, "Besides, they
don't know our secret, do they?"

It was certainly true. These five shared a very
special secret, indeed.

Appelemando's dreams!

You see, whenever he daydreamed with his friends, they could actually SEE the dreams! Right out of the top of his head they drifted. They twisted through shafts of brilliant sunlight. Floated up, up, up into the sunny sky. There was so much to look at, animals, birds, flowers . . . all in wondrous, vibrant colors!

Appelemando enjoyed dreaming just for them.
He did big dreams.
He did tall dreams.
He did little dreams.
He did middle dreams.

One day, Lark announced, "Let's capture one of Appelemando's dreams on a piece of paper! Then we could look at it even when Appelemando isn't around!"

The children tried and tried to get the dreams to stay, but each time the dreams drifted off and disappeared. Then Petra and Dorma covered a piece of paper with water from the well tub they had been playing in. At that very instant, a dream floated up from Appelemando's head, and Lark and Jefftoe pushed the paper in front of it. It held fast.

"Hurray," they exclaimed for joy. "Now we can keep his dreams forever!"

It wasn't long before they discovered that Appelemando's dreams would stay on anything that was moist or damp.

Mops drying over balcony rails.

Laundry airing on clotheslines.

Bottoms of fat, white ducks waddling up the street.

"Boy, Appelemando," Jefftoe laughed, "you better not ever dream on a rainy day."

"What a mess we'd have," Lark snickered. "Lucky you only dream on sunny days!"

71

Then, one day when Appelemando had begun to dream, the sun suddenly hid behind gray storm clouds. The wind blustered, and rain dropped from the clouds above them.

"Oh no!" Lark squealed. "What are we going to do?"

"Appelemando, don't dream anymore," Jefftoe ordered.

"You just can't," Petra and Dorma said, as they were pelted with wet raindrops.

Lark clapped Appelemando's hat tight onto his head, but it was no use. The dream had already drifted up and was floating toward the buildings of the town.

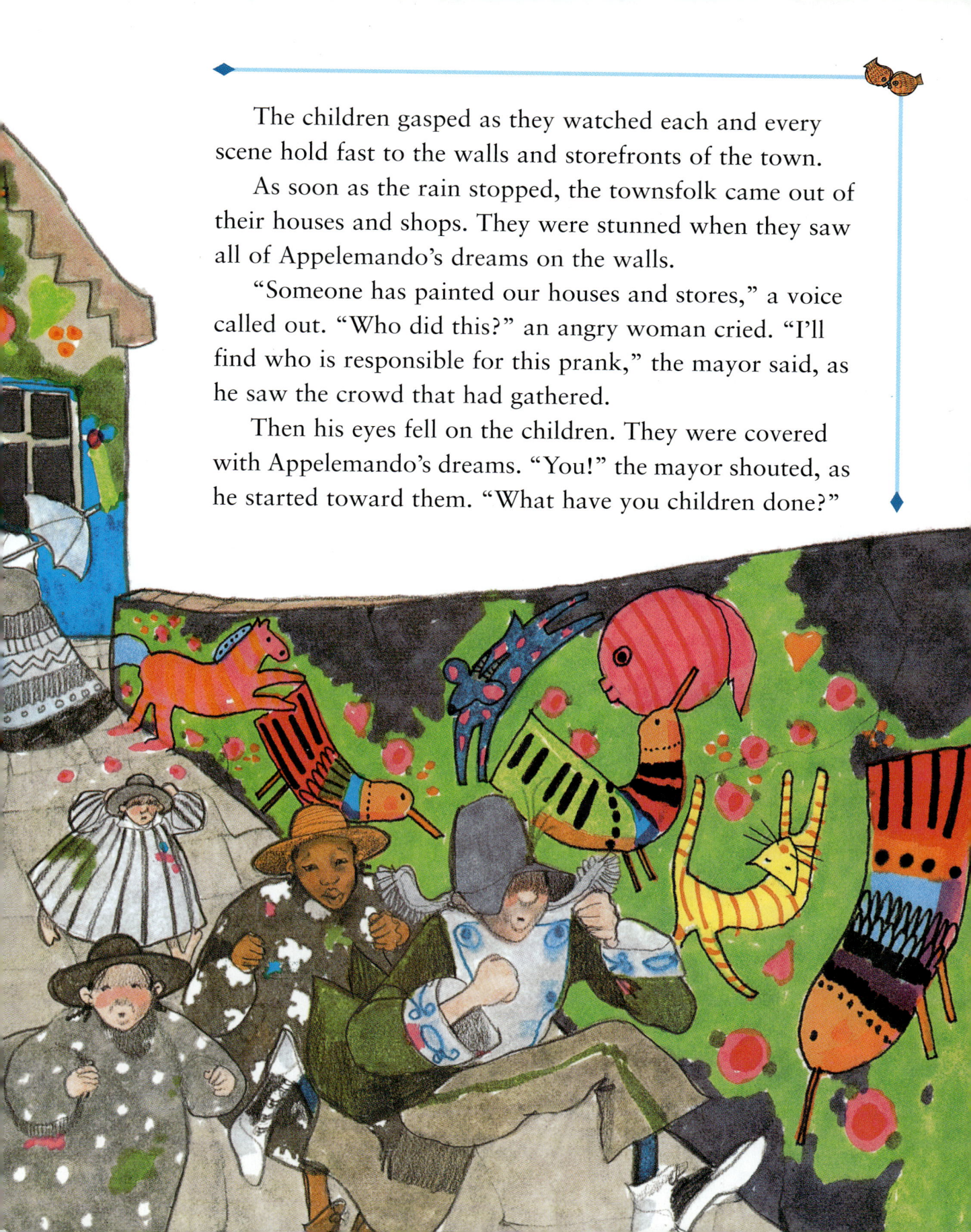

The children gasped as they watched each and every scene hold fast to the walls and storefronts of the town.

As soon as the rain stopped, the townsfolk came out of their houses and shops. They were stunned when they saw all of Appelemando's dreams on the walls.

"Someone has painted our houses and stores," a voice called out. "Who did this?" an angry woman cried. "I'll find who is responsible for this prank," the mayor said, as he saw the crowd that had gathered.

Then his eyes fell on the children. They were covered with Appelemando's dreams. "You!" the mayor shouted, as he started toward them. "What have you children done?"

The children were taken to the elders of the village.

"Do you mean to tell us that all of those things on our walls are dreams?" they asked when the children explained.

The more the children tried to tell the villagers about Appelemando's wonderful dreams, the more suspicious the elders became.

"If what you say is true, let's see Appelemando dream right now. Here in this place," the mayor snapped.

The elders leaned forward in their seats and watched Appelemando.

But the harder Appelemando tried to dream, the more impossible it became. Nothing at all would come into his mind.

Jefftoe, Lark, Petra, and Dorma all stared at the air above Appelemando's head waiting, waiting, but nothing appeared.

"I knew they were lying," a villager whispered.

"You should be ashamed of yourselves . . . such a ridiculous story," one elder said out loud.

"Let them scrub the walls," a voice rang out. "Fit punishment for painting our village without our permission!"

As the children walked toward home after the ordeal, they were afraid that Appelemando's wonderful dreams would never happen again. They walked and worried. In their sadness, they didn't watch the path. When they looked up, they were in the middle of the forest.

They had lost their way.

As hours passed, the children's families became more and more alarmed. They alerted all the people in the village, who sent out search parties to look for the children. "Where could they be?" they all pondered.

"Our people will never find us here," Petra and Dorma cried.

"They won't even know where to look," Jefftoe said sadly.

"If only we could signal them somehow," Lark said thoughtfully.

Then all of the children looked at Appelemando.

"You can help, Appelemando," Lark announced. "If you dream a dream big and bright enough, it will rise above the trees. People in the village will see it and know we are here."

"Yeah!" they all cheered.

But Appelemando was quiet. "I can't dream anymore," he cried.

"You have to try," they all said. "You must!"

All Appelemando could think of were the bitter words of the elders, the people who didn't believe him, and try as he might, nothing would appear in his mind. There was no dream.

Then he looked into the eyes of his friends. In Lark's eyes there was certainty. In Jefftoe's, steady sureness. In Petra's and Dorma's, complete expectation, for they loved his dreams.

Then he closed his eyes and began to see.

Bright colors of every hue, shape, and texture floated from the top of Appelemando's head. They twisted through the air. The wind caught them and lifted them above the trees.

Sure enough, the villagers saw the dream just above the forest where the children were. They all followed this vision and when they found the children, they wept for joy. Never again would they question the importance of dreams.

Now the village is no longer a drab place. The path leading to it is bustling with visitors drawn there by rich colors and soaring images that cover the walls of the town. Colorful scenes that its townsfolk are very proud of, indeed.

It is a dreamy place.

A wonderful place.

An old man sits by the fountain in the square. An old man who loves to dream. For him, dreams are magic chariots pulled through his mind by galloping hues of color. For him, dreaming is a way of life.

PATRICIA POLACCO

Patricia Polacco grew up in a family of artists and storytellers. Perhaps it was only natural that she became both! Although she did not begin her career as an author and illustrator until she was forty-one, she has always been a collector of stories.

Every morning, Patricia Polacco sits in one of the many rocking chairs she has in her home. She rocks and rocks until her imagination begins to soar. In her mind, she pictures the stories she will write. By the time she is ready to put them down on paper, they seem to pour right onto the page. Maybe that's how Patricia Polacco got the idea for *Appelemando's Dreams*!

"My fondest memories are of sitting around a stove or open fire, eating apples and popping corn while listening to the old ones tell glorious stories about their homeland and the past. " — Patricia Polacco

Response Corner

WRITE A POEM

If You Can't Say Something Nice...

People often feel good or bad because of how others treat them. At the end of the story, the villagers are proud of Appelemando and his dreams. How do you think he feels? Write a poem that describes how you feel when someone is proud of you. Share your poem with your family or your classmates.

DRAW A SCENE

Skywriting

Appelemando made his village more beautiful. You can make your classroom more beautiful. Place a sheet of plastic wrap against a window and smooth out the bubbles. Work with a partner to draw a dream, using brightly colored markers. Look at the dreams other students have made. Write one or two sentences about how the scenes make your classroom look.

WRITE A PARAGRAPH

Paid to Dream

Many people use imagination in their jobs. With two classmates, list some jobs in which a person would need to have a good imagination. Then choose the job you would most like to do, and write a paragraph that tells why.

What Do You Think?

♦ How do Appelemando's dreams change the village?

♦ Who is the old man at the end of the story? If you could ask him one question, what would it be?

♦ Name one or two ways you could make *your* community more beautiful.

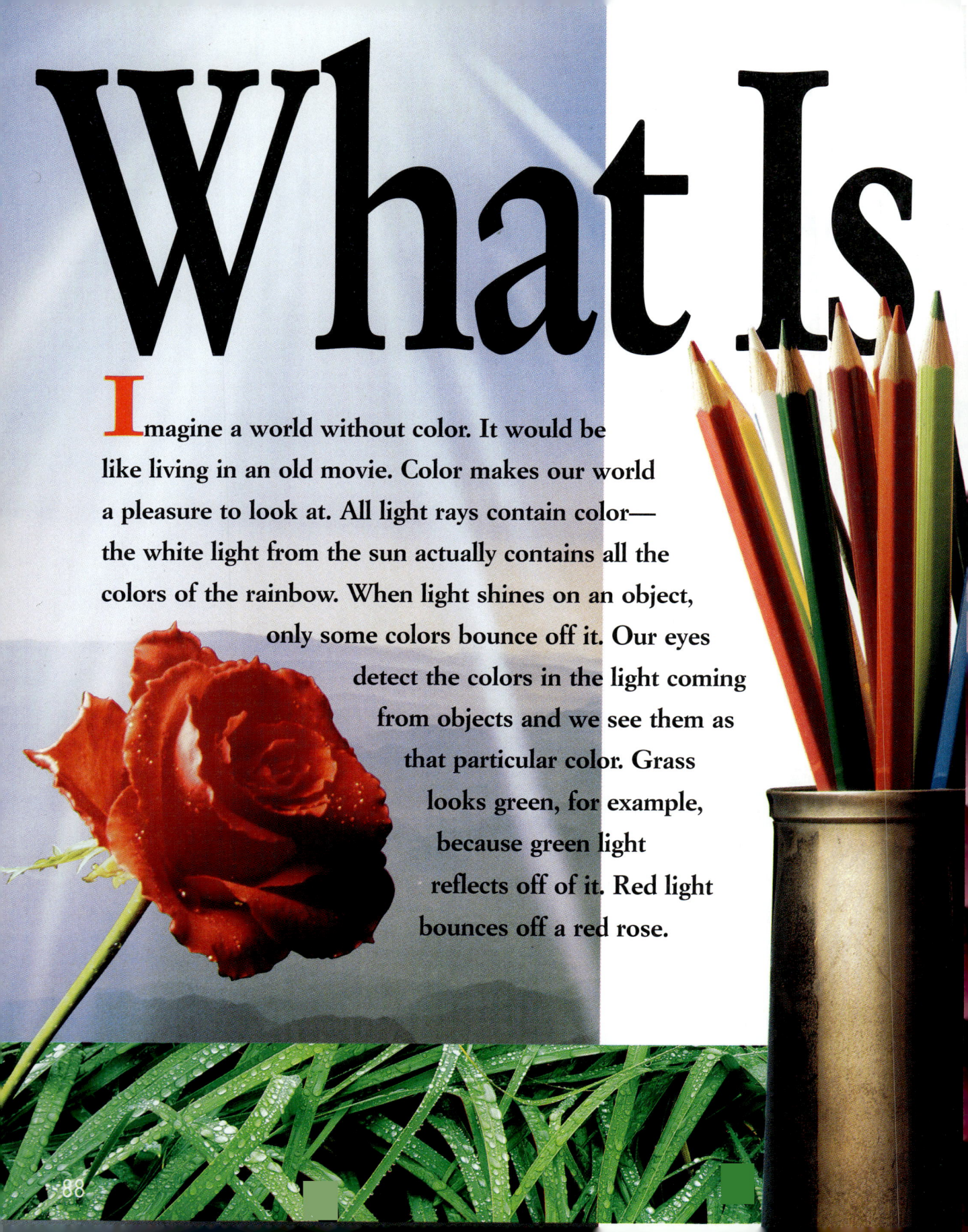

What Is

Imagine a world without color. It would be like living in an old movie. Color makes our world a pleasure to look at. All light rays contain color— the white light from the sun actually contains all the colors of the rainbow. When light shines on an object, only some colors bounce off it. Our eyes detect the colors in the light coming from objects and we see them as that particular color. Grass looks green, for example, because green light reflects off of it. Red light bounces off a red rose.

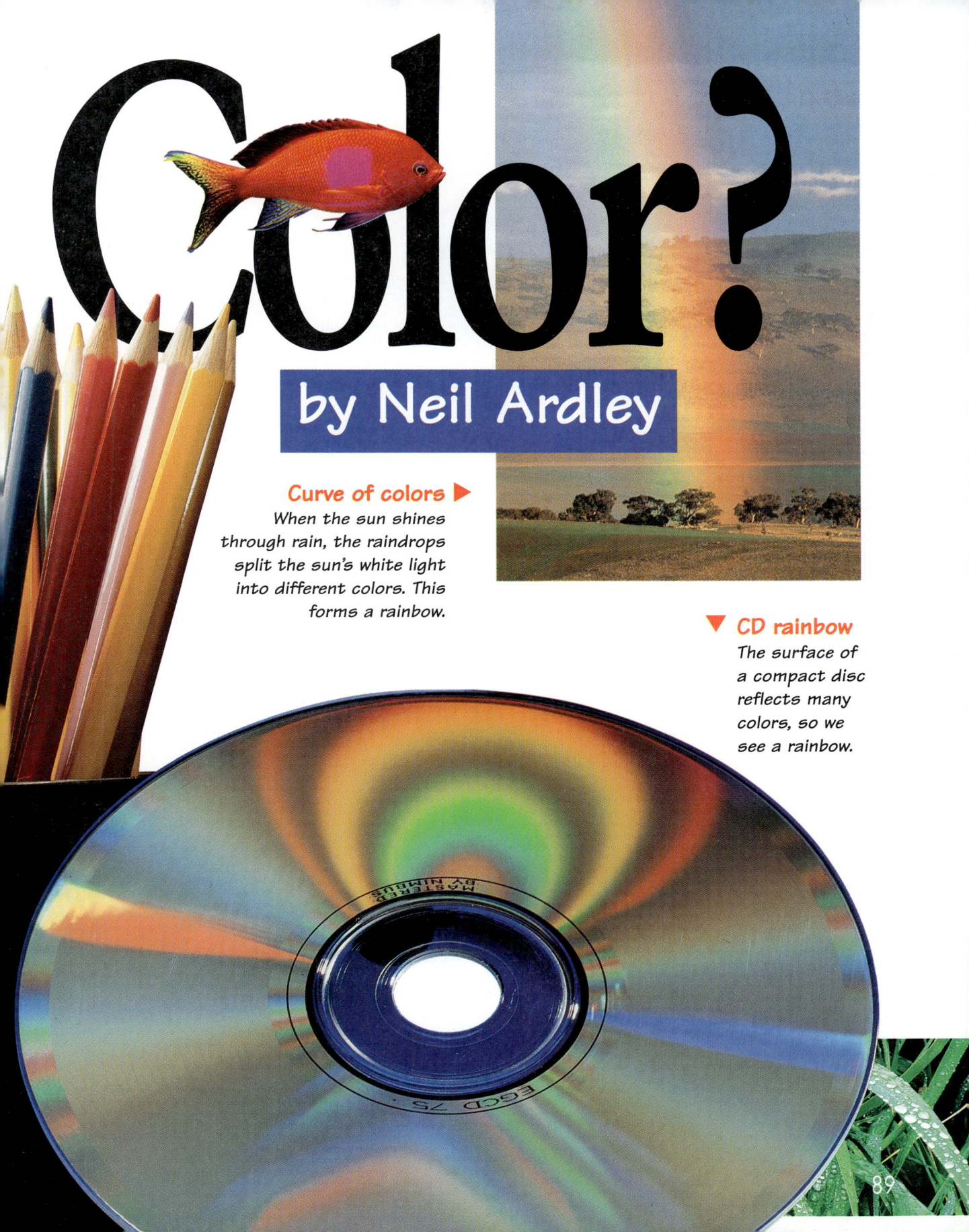

Color?

by Neil Ardley

Curve of colors ▶
When the sun shines through rain, the raindrops split the sun's white light into different colors. This forms a rainbow.

▼ CD rainbow
The surface of a compact disc reflects many colors, so we see a rainbow.

Sunset

The sky often looks orange or red when the sun sets. Find out why the sky changes color by making an orange and red sunset using a flashlight, milk, and water.▼

Water
(two cups)

Flashlight

Milk
(two tablespoons)

Red sky at night

White light from the sun passes through the air. At sunset, only orange and red rays get through the air. Tiny particles of dust or smoke in the air stop all the other colors. The sun looks orange-red and it lights up the clouds with an orange-red color.

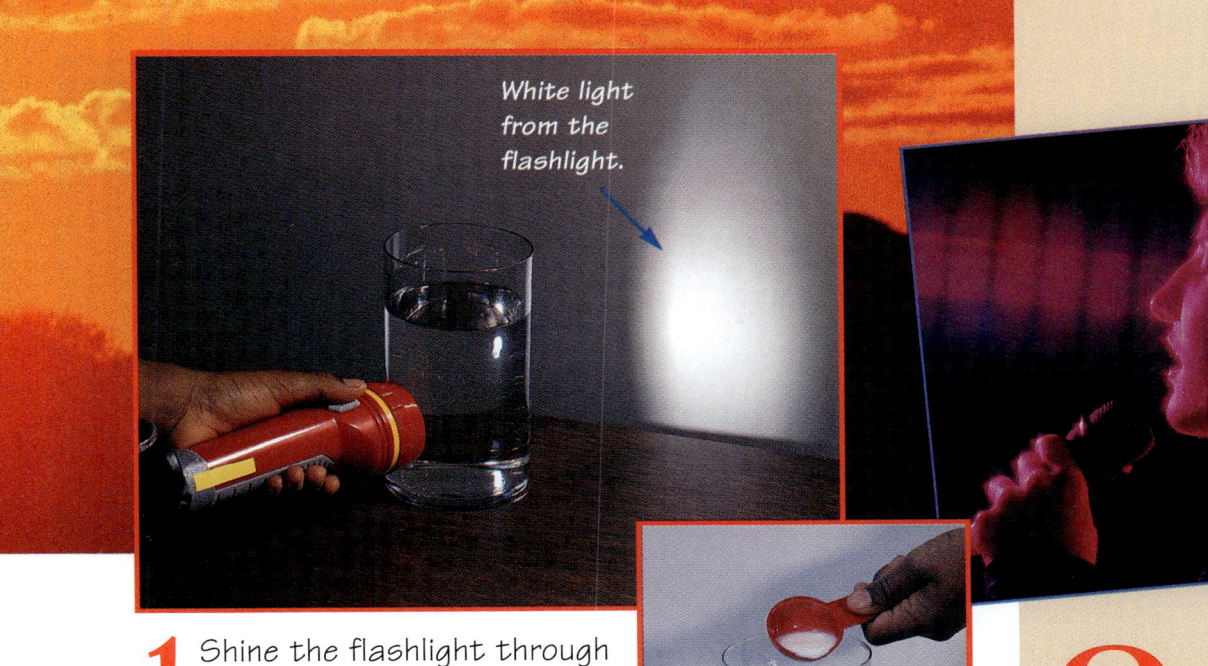

White light from the flashlight.

1 Shine the flashlight through the water onto a white wall. It gives off a white light.

2 Add milk to the water.

3 Now shine the flashlight through the white milky water. The wall lights up with an orange-red color!

The milky water stops some colors in the light from getting through.

Only orange and red light rays pass through the milky water to reach the wall.

On stage

Stage lamps produce bright beams of colored light to create fantastic effects. In each lamp, white light from a bulb passes through a plastic sheet of a certain color. The plastic stops all the colors but one in the white light and lets only that color pass through.

91

Hidden Colors

Some colors are not what they seem. You can show that they are made of lots of different colors mixed together. It's easy to find the hidden colors in the inks in felt-tipped pens.

Coffee filters also work.

1 Cut the blotting paper into strips.

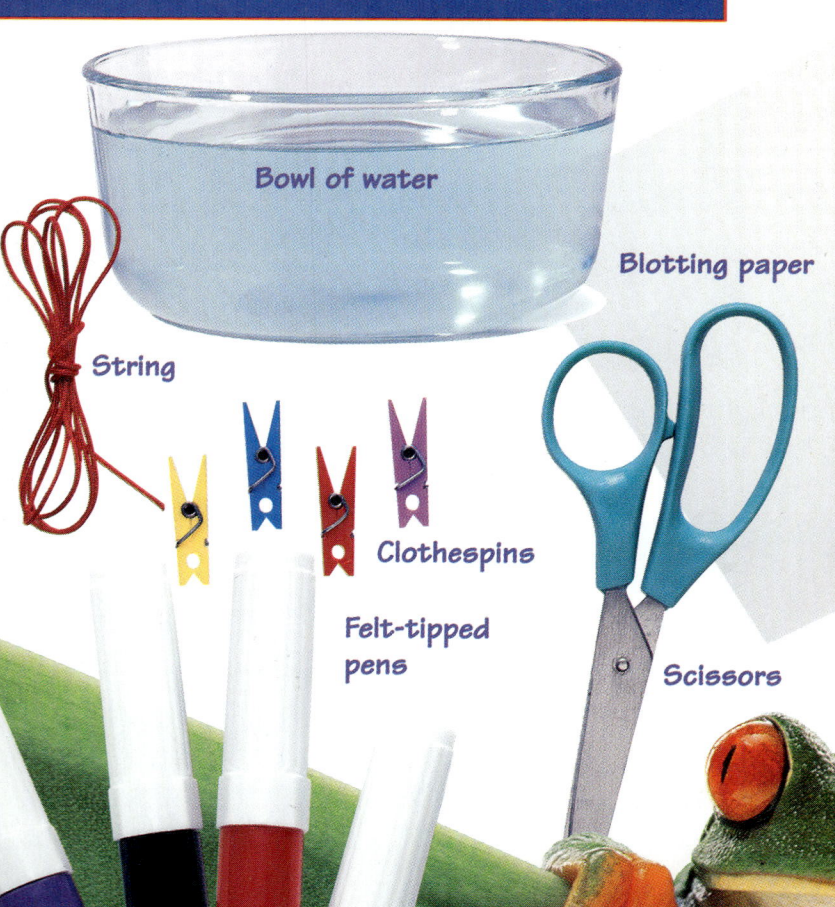

Bowl of water

Blotting paper

String

Clothespins

Felt-tipped pens

Scissors

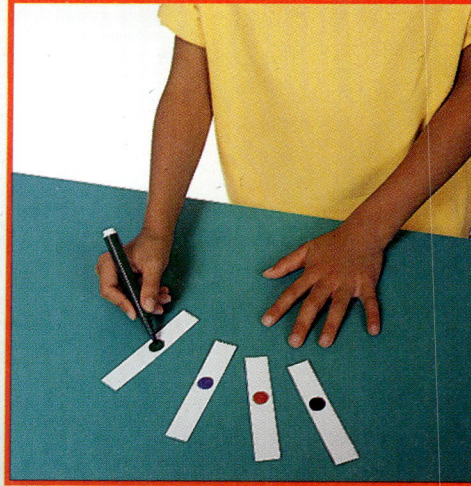

2 Draw a circle of a different color near the bottom of each strip.

3 Tie the string to some supports to keep it in place above the bowl. Attach the strips of paper to the string. Arrange them so that the water touches the bottom edges but does not reach the ink.

Leave space between the water and the ink.

4 The water moves up the paper. Colors move different distances with the water, and each ink may separate into several colors.

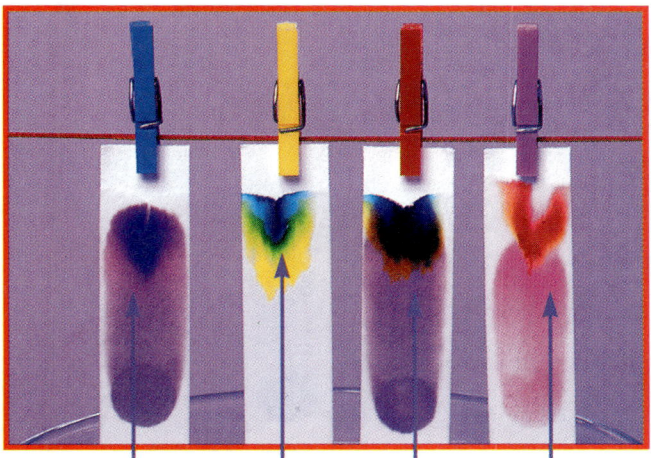

This *purple* ink contains no hidden colors.

This *green* ink contains blue and yellow.

This black ink contains many colors.

This *red* ink contains no hidden colors.

Making paints

Paints come in many different shades of color, but in fact they contain hidden colors. Paints are made by mixing pigments of several basic colors together in different amounts. Artists mix paints together in a similar way when they paint a picture.

How many colors?

Pictures in books contain three colored inks plus a black ink.

- Magenta
- Yellow
- Blue
- Black

ZENY'

from *National Geographic World* magazine

How did the zebra get its stripes? Zeny Fuentes painted them . . . just as he painted pink fur on the coyote in his hands and polka dots on the armadillo. Zeny lives in Oaxaca (wə•häk´ə), a state in Mexico. Woodcarvers there are famous for their art—colorful creatures in bold shapes. At school Zeny, seventeen, didn't study art, but he is already a well-known artist.

He has traveled to the United States to show his work at a gallery in Kansas City, Missouri.

Copal Cat is carved of copal wood.

"I learned how to carve from my father and grandfather," Zeny says. He uses simple tools such as a pocket knife and a larger knife called a machete (mə•shet´ē). Zeny started carving when he was eight. "At first my pieces looked stiff and rough," he recalls. "Now I can give the animals more personality." Zeny carves animals he has seen in his village, in books, or on television. But he paints most of them in colors that, he says, are "pure fantasy."

Armadillo
*has a fabulous
suit of armor.*

Anteater:
Fantástico!

Zeny's Zebra
*has a rope
mane.*

95

Jerry Pinkney:
Achiever of Dreams

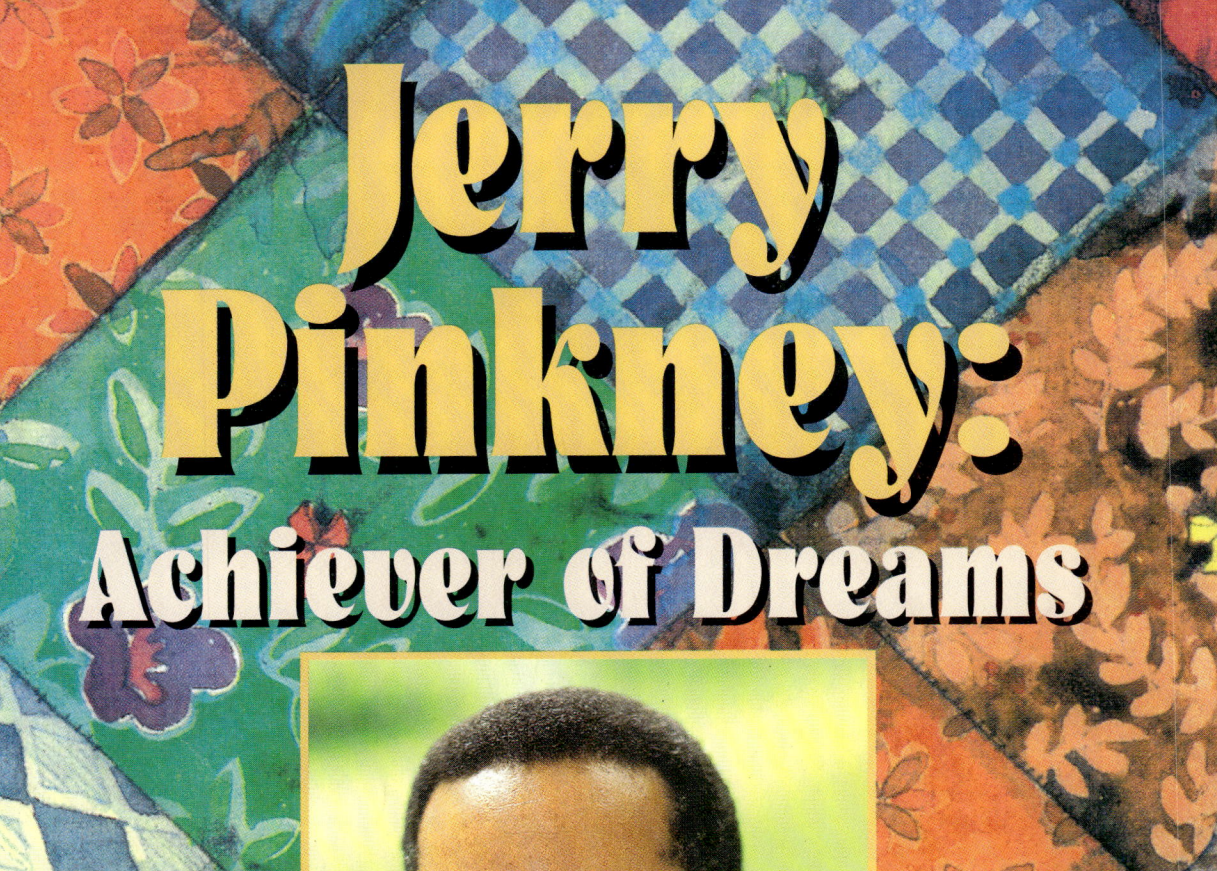

Jerry Pinkney's artwork can be seen in dozens of children's books. Read about his lifelong dream and how it came true.

Award-Winning
Author

by Ilene Cooper

Bright Beginnings

As a young boy, Jerry Pinkney enjoyed watching his two older brothers draw pictures. He often tried to imitate them. Today, boys and girls might try to imitate Jerry Pinkney's drawings, because Jerry became a famous artist.

"I was always interested in drawing," Jerry Pinkney remembers. "I started out drawing anything that had wheels—cars, trucks, fire engines. By the time I was in school, I was always the class artist. It was kind of magical to be the kid who could draw."

When Jerry was eleven, he had a job selling newspapers on a street corner in his hometown of Philadelphia. The job wasn't very entertaining, so he made sure he always brought along a pad of paper and a pencil. He sketched anything that stood still.

Unfortunately, many of those early drawings weren't saved. "I wish I had more of them," he says. "I remember some of those early drawings and paintings, and I'd love to see them again. In those days, kids' drawings were not the kinds of things people kept."

While selling papers, Jerry met John Liney, the cartoonist of the "Henry" cartoon strip. Liney was the first person to help Jerry get started in his career. He took Jerry to visit his studio, and he sometimes gave Jerry different materials to work with. It was exciting for Jerry to meet and work with a real cartoonist. But even more important, Liney's success was proof that somebody could make a living as an artist.

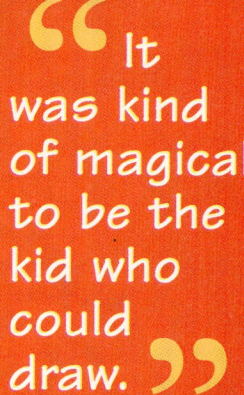

"It was kind of magical to be the kid who could draw."

◀ Jerry Pinkney at age six

▲ Jerry painted this picture when he was seven. He named it *Boy with a Wagon*.

In 1939, when Jerry was born, the television was not as common as it is now. He thinks the lack of television was good for his imagination. Though he doesn't remember listening to popular fairy tales, he heard many stories at home. He used his imagination to create pictures in his own mind.

The Early Career Years

Jerry went to a special high school called Dobbins Vocational High School. There, he took a commercial art course, and he learned design and illustration. After school, he worked at a sign painting

◀ Jerry's high school graduation, 1957

business run by one of his teachers. "My mom was very supportive of my artwork," he says, "and my dad was too, but he was less sure it was something that could be a career."

Still, it was his father who opened Jerry's eyes to the world of color. "My dad was a house painter, and I used to go down to the paint store with him and watch him match and mix colors. . . . During those days the paint store was where art supplies were sold, so it was always a fun place to be."

There weren't many books in Jerry's house during his childhood, but there were lots of magazines, and he loved to study them. "I used to look at the photo magazines like *Life* and *Look* and read the ads. That was the kind of work I did after I graduated from the Philadelphia Museum College of Art. I began drawing greeting cards and advertising. . . .

Those experiences taught me a lot."

Career Words

Models are people who pose for artists or photographers.

Advertising, in the art world, is using art and design to help sell things.

Narrative art is art that tells a story.

Commercial art is artwork created to be sold for profit.

Projects are problems to solve, tasks, or pieces of work someone plans to do.

Design is the arrangement of different parts, such as words and pictures on a page, so that they look pleasing.

Publishing is the printing of someone's work to sell to the public.

Illustration is the use of pictures to explain or decorate.

Watercolor is a type of painting done in colors that are mixed with water.

▲ Jerry Pinkney at work in his home studio

By this time, Jerry, his wife Gloria, and their young family were living in Boston, where there were many publishing houses and a large children's book industry. Many people he met there encouraged Jerry to try illustrating children's books.

Designing advertising, illustrating textbooks, even working on greeting cards helped when he began his book illustration career. Jerry's first book was *The Adventures of Spider*, a collection of West African folktales. He thinks his break into book illustration came because interest in African American writers was growing. "I think there was an awareness, if not pressure, that the African American artist could perhaps bring something unique to a text, something more personal."

When Jerry receives a story from a publisher, he starts to think about what pictures will help tell the story, how to place the art and the text, and how the type should look on the page. His work is usually done in pencil and watercolor, but he might use color pencils as well.

How does he decide what pictures will be best to illustrate a story? Jerry says, "My interest is in narrative art. It's very important to me that the pictures tell the story. This idea guides me, because if

> **" It's very important to me that the pictures tell the story. "**

I've drawn a picture, and it isn't necessary to tell the story, that's a picture that won't be used. The art should work in such a way that even a child who can't read can follow the action."

The Present . . . and the Future

Jerry has become successful enough to be able to pick and choose the projects he works on. He likes to keep a balance in his work. If he's been drawing stories with lots of animals, he begins choosing projects that feature humans. When he draws his characters, he often uses people he knows as models. For instance, his wife, Gloria, was the model for the mother in *The Patchwork Quilt*.

When Jerry started working as a book illustrator, there

Jerry and Gloria ▶
Pinkney today

were very few African American artists doing this kind of work. "Things have changed unbelievably. Now, there are many books that feature African American characters, and there are many wonderful Black artists drawing them."

Jerry used his wife, Gloria, as his ▶
model for this illustration in the
book *The Patchwork Quilt.*

One of those artists is Jerry's own son Brian, who is also a well-known children's book illustrator. Jerry encouraged all of his children —his other sons, Myles and Scott, and his daughter, Troy —to get involved with art. In one way or another, they all use their artistic talents in their careers. Jerry also made sure he and his wife kept *all* of the kids' artwork, so that, unlike their dad, they'll be able to look at their earliest drawings. Now, the Pinkneys are collecting the pictures their grandchildren draw.

▲ Jerry Pinkney's son Brian and his wife, Andrea, worked together to write and illustrate the award-winning book *Dear Benjamin Banneker.*

Have you read any of these books? They are just a sampling of Jerry Pinkney's work.

Meet Ilene Cooper

I have three jobs. During the day I am a children's book editor at a magazine. I help review about 2,500 books a year for school and public librarians. A book review is like a book report. Can you imagine doing 2,500 book reports a year? It's a lot of work, but I love to see all the new books as they come in.

At night I sit down to write my own books. I have written many books for children, including novels for teens and several books of nonfiction.

Because so much of my career is centered around children's books, I was asked to do the interviews for this anthology. It was great fun to interview the authors and illustrators, since so many of them are heroes of mine. I also got lots of good ideas from them that will help me with my own writing. Almost all the people I interviewed said how important reading was to them when they were children.

When I was a child, there were two things I loved to do— read and play with paper dolls. Reading gave me a love for words. It also showed me that characters in books could be as real as the people I met every day. Playing with paper dolls was a way of telling myself stories. Now, I can still do what I've always loved. I can read books, write books, and tell stories.

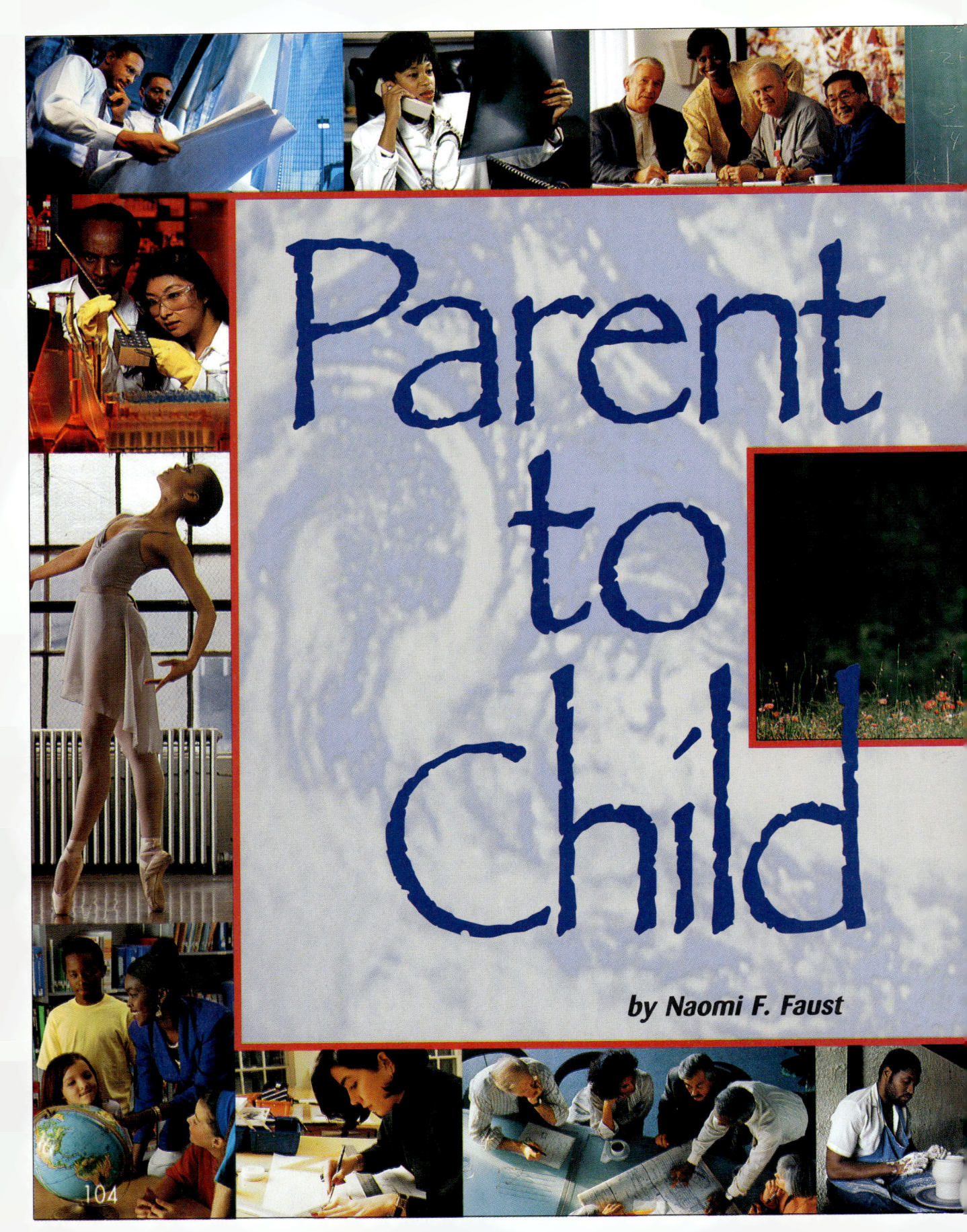

Parent to Child

by Naomi F. Faust

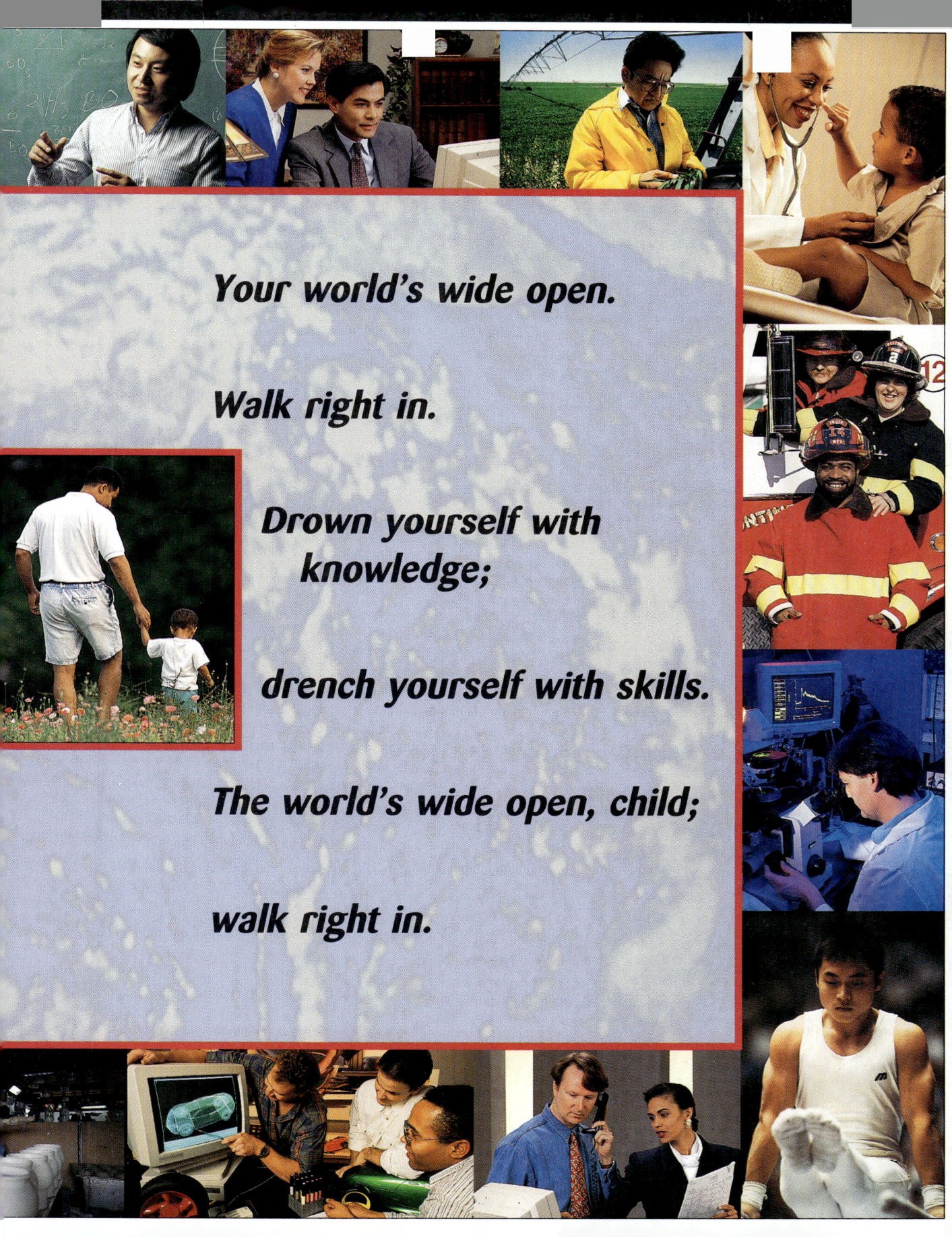

Your world's wide open.

Walk right in.

Drown yourself with
knowledge;

drench yourself with skills.

The world's wide open, child;

walk right in.

Response

Good Advice

The poem "Parent to Child" sounds like something Jerry Pinkney might say to his own children. He would probably agree with the poem's ideas. Read the poem again. Then list some skills *you* might want to learn someday. Use your imagination!

DRAW CHARACTERS

Pictures of Imagination

Jerry Pinkney's family was fond of telling stories. Read a story aloud to your classmates, but don't show them the pictures. When you've finished reading, ask your listeners to draw their favorite characters. Have them share their pictures and tell what story clues they used to draw the characters.

Corner

SHARE A PHOTO

Every Picture Tells a Story

Jerry Pinkney uses pictures to tell a story. News magazines also use pictures to tell stories. Look through several news magazines. Choose a photo that tells a story. Share it with a small group. Discuss why the photographer chose to show the persons or things in the photo.

What Do You Think?

❋ Describe Jerry Pinkney's career. How did he begin? How did he become successful?

❋ Jerry Pinkney's father was not sure his son could make enough money as an artist. Why might Jerry's father have thought as he did?

❋ Some people have a talent for drawing and painting. What other kinds of talents do people have?

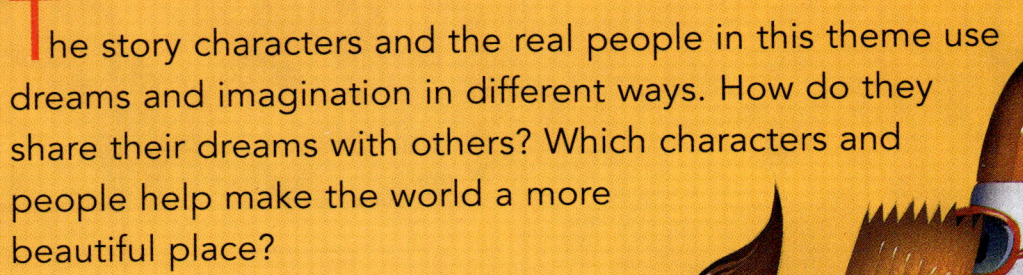

The story characters and the real people in this theme use dreams and imagination in different ways. How do they share their dreams with others? Which characters and people help make the world a more beautiful place?

Appelemando has big dreams and middle dreams, tall dreams and small dreams. What kind of dreams does Jerry Pinkney have? Explain your answer.

ACTIVITY CORNER

What are your dreams for the future? What places would you like to see? What would you like to do? Make a painting or a diorama that shows a place you would like to see in the future. Show yourself doing something there.

THEME WRAP-UP

Discovering Courage

How do you find courage when you need it? Can other people help you be brave? The characters in this theme find the answers to these questions. Maybe they will help you find courage, too!

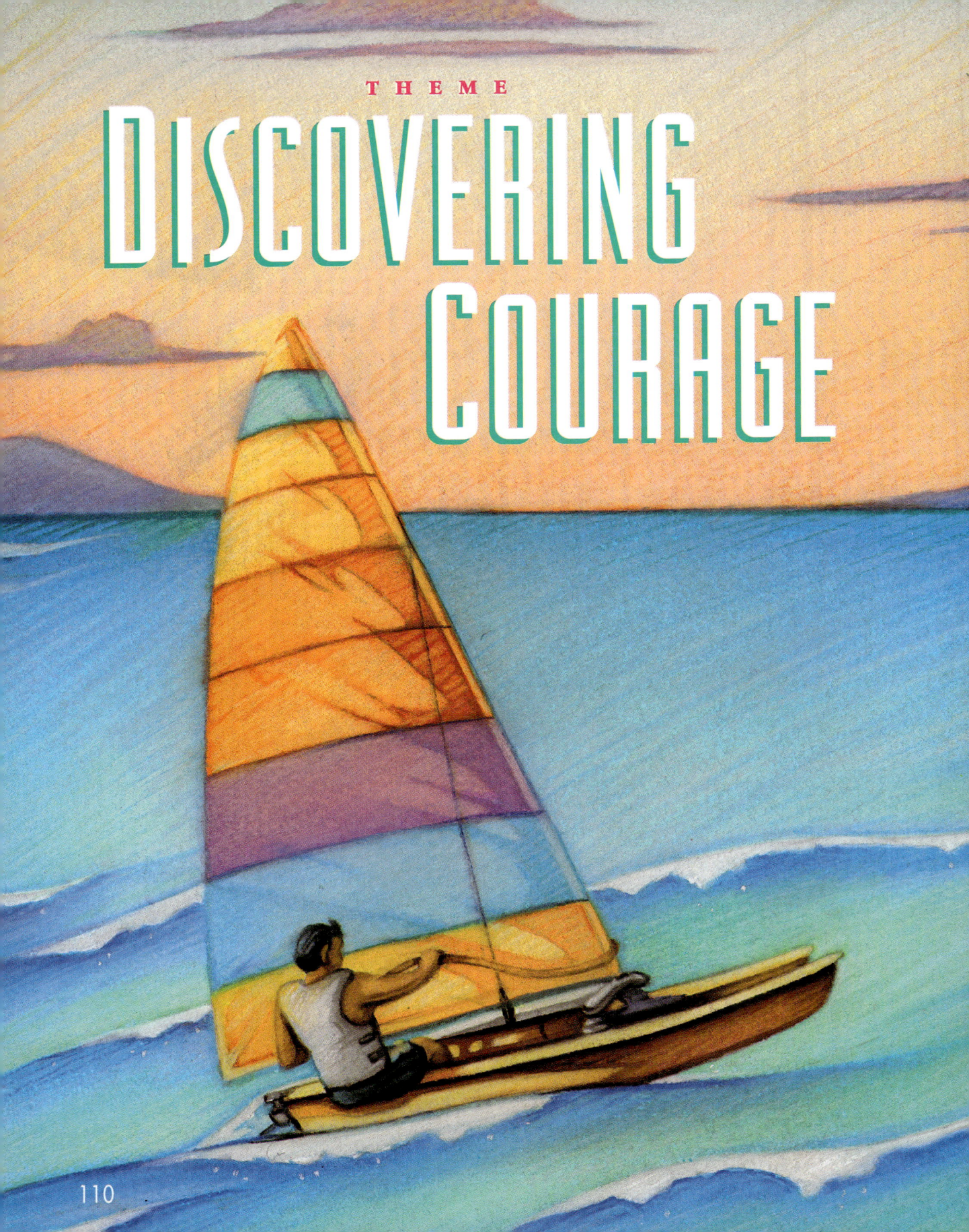

CONTENTS

Brave Irene
written and illustrated by William Steig

Storm in the Night
by Mary Stolz

The Mystery of the Sounds in the Night
by Joan Lowery Nixon

A wolf . . .
Teton Sioux Song

When I Wake
by Jonathan London

Art and Literature
The Diving Board
by Norman Rockwell

Lester's Dog
by Karen Hesse

Think Positive!
from Current Health 1 *magazine*

My Name Is María Isabel
by Alma Flor Ada

How a Girl Got Her Chinese Name
by Nellie Wong

BOOKSHELF

Frida María
by Deborah Nourse Lattimore

Frida finds the courage to be true to herself—the best Frida there ever was!

Award-Winning Author and Illustrator
Signatures Library

The Wave
by Margaret Hodges

One man's courage and quick thinking save an entire Japanese village from ruin.

New York Times Best Illustrated Book; Caldecott Honor
Signatures Library

Ramona the Brave
by Beverly Cleary

Ramona bravely faces new teachers, new books, a new bedroom, and a mean dog!

Children's Choice

Annie and the Old One
by Miska Miles

Annie needs true, lasting courage to face a very sad time in her life.

Newbery Honor

The Magic Fan
written and illustrated by Keith Baker

Yoshi finds a magic fan and saves a town from a tidal wave.

SLJ Best Books; Notable Trade Book in Social Studies

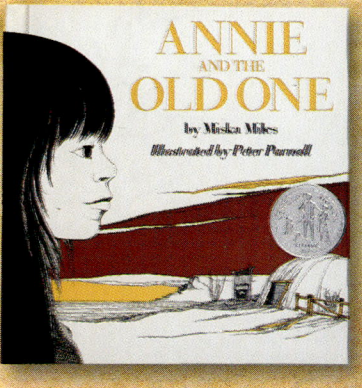

Brave

Brave Irene
by William Steig

New York
Times Best
Illustrated Book

Notable Trade
Book for the
Language Arts

Irene

by
William Steig

Mrs. Bobbin, the dressmaker, was tired and had a bad headache, but she still managed to sew the last stitches in the gown she was making.

"It's the most beautiful dress in the whole world!" said her daughter, Irene. "The duchess will love it."

"It *is* nice," her mother admitted. "But, dumpling, it's for tonight's ball, and I don't have the strength to bring it. I feel sick."

"Poor Mama," said Irene. "I can get it there!"

"No, cupcake, I can't let you," said Mrs. Bobbin. "Such a huge package, and it's such a long way to the palace. Besides, it's starting to snow."

"But I *love* snow," Irene insisted. She coaxed her mother into bed, covered her with two quilts, and added a blanket for her feet. Then she fixed her some tea with lemon and honey and put more wood in the stove.

With great care, Irene took the splendid gown down from the dummy and packed it in a big box with plenty of tissue paper.

"Dress warmly, pudding," her mother called in a weak voice, "and don't forget to button up. It's cold out there, and windy."

Irene put on her fleece-lined boots, her red hat and muffler, her heavy coat, and her mittens. She kissed her mother's hot forehead six times, then once again, made sure she was tucked in snugly, and slipped out with the big box, shutting the door firmly behind her.

It really was cold outside, very cold. The wind whirled the falling snowflakes about, this way, that way, and into Irene's squinting face. She set out on the uphill path to Farmer Bennett's sheep pasture.

By the time she got there, the snow was up to her ankles and the wind was worse. It hurried her along and made her stumble. Irene resented this; the box was problem enough. "Easy does it!" she cautioned the wind, leaning back hard against it.

By the middle of the pasture, the flakes were falling thicker. Now the wind drove Irene along so rudely she had to hop, skip, and go helter-skeltering over the knobby ground. Cold snow sifted into her boots and chilled her feet. She pushed out her lip and hurried on. This was an important errand.

When she reached Apple Road, the wind decided to put on a show. It ripped branches from trees and flung them about, swept up and scattered the fallen snow, got in front of Irene to keep her from moving ahead. Irene turned around and pressed on backwards.

"Go home!" the wind squalled. "Irene . . . go hooooooome . . ."

"I will do no such thing," she snapped. "No such thing, you wicked wind!"

"Go ho–o–ome," the wind yodeled. "GO HO–WO–WOME," it shrieked, "or else." For a short second, Irene wondered if she shouldn't heed the wind's warning. But no! *The gown had to get to the duchess!*

The wind wrestled her for the package—walloped it, twisted it, shook it, snatched at it. But Irene wouldn't yield. "It's my mother's work!" she screamed.

Then—oh, woe!—the box was wrenched from her mittened grasp and sent bumbling along in the snow. Irene went after it.

She pounced and took hold, but the ill-tempered wind
ripped the box open. The ball gown flounced out and went
waltzing through the powdered air with tissue-paper attendants.

Irene clung to the empty box and watched the beautiful gown
disappear.

How could anything so terribly wrong be allowed to
happen? Tears froze on her lashes. Her dear mother's hard
work, all those days of measuring, cutting, pinning, stitching . . .
for *this*? And the poor duchess! Irene decided she would
have to trudge on with just the box and explain everything in
person.

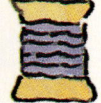

She went shuffling through the snow. Would her mother understand, she wondered, that it was the wind's fault, not hers? Would the duchess be angry? The wind was howling like a wild animal.

Suddenly Irene stepped in a hole and fell over with a twisted ankle. She blamed it on the wind. "Keep quiet!" she scolded. "You've done enough damage already. You've spoiled everything! *Everything!*" The wind swallowed up her words.

She sat in the snow in great pain, afraid she wouldn't be able to go on. But she managed to get to her feet and start moving. It hurt. Home, where she longed to be, where she and her mother could be warm together, was far behind. It's got to be closer to the palace, she thought. But where any place was in all this snow, she couldn't be sure.

She plowed on, dragging furrows with her sore foot. The short winter day was almost done.

Am I still going the right way, she wondered. There was no one around to advise her. Whoever else there was in this snow-covered world was far, far away, and safe indoors—even the animals in their burrows. She went plodding on.

Soon night took over. She knew in the dark that the muffled snow was still falling—she could feel it. She was cold and alone in the middle of nowhere. Irene was lost.

She had to keep moving. She was hoping she'd come to a house, any house at all, and be taken in. She badly needed to be in someone's arms. The snow was above her knees now. She shoved her way through it, clutching the empty box.

She was asking how long a small person could keep this struggle up, when she realized it was getting lighter. There was a soft glow coming from somewhere below her.

She waded toward this glow, and soon was gazing down a long slope at a brightly lit mansion. It had to be the palace!

Irene pushed forward with all her strength and—*sloosh!*
thwump!—she plunged downward and was buried. She had
fallen off a little cliff. Only her hat and the box in her hands
stuck out above the snow.

Even if she could call for help, no one would hear her. Her
body shook. Her teeth chattered. Why not freeze to death, she
thought, and let all these troubles end. Why not? She was
already buried.

And never see her mother's face again? Her good mother
who smelled like fresh-baked bread? In an explosion of fury,
she flung her body about to free herself and was finally able to
climb up on her knees and look around.

How to get down to that glittering palace? As soon as she raised the question, she had the answer.

She laid the box down and climbed aboard. But it pressed into the snow and stuck. She tried again, and this time, instead of climbing on, she leaped. The box shot forward, like a sled.

The wind raced after Irene but couldn't keep up. In a moment she would be with people again, inside where it was warm. The sled slowed and jerked to a stop on paving stones.

The time had come to break the bad news to the duchess. With the empty box clasped to her chest, Irene strode nervously toward the palace.

But then her feet stopped moving and her mouth fell open. She stared. Maybe this was impossible, yet there it was, a little way off and over to the right, hugging the trunk of a tree—the beautiful ball gown! The wind was holding it there.

"Mama!" Irene shouted. "Mama, I found it!"

She managed somehow, despite the wind's meddling, to get the gown off the tree and back in its box. And in another moment she was at the door of the palace. She knocked twice with the big brass knocker. The door opened and she burst in.

She was welcomed by cheering servants and a delirious duchess. They couldn't believe she had come over the mountain in such a storm, all by herself. She had to tell the whole story, every detail. And she did.

Then she asked to be taken right back to her sick mother. But it was out of the question, they said; the road that ran around the mountain wouldn't be cleared till morning.

"Don't fret, child," said the duchess. "Your mother is surely sleeping now. We'll get you there first thing tomorrow."

Irene was given a good dinner as she sat by the fire, the moisture steaming off her clothes. The duchess, meanwhile, got into her freshly ironed gown before the guests began arriving in their sleighs.

What a wonderful ball it was! The duchess in her new gown was like a bright star in the sky. Irene in her ordinary dress was radiant. She was swept up into dances by handsome aristocrats, who kept her feet off the floor to spare her ankle. Her mother would enjoy hearing all about it.

Early the next morning, when snow had long since ceased falling, Mrs. Bobbin woke from a good night's sleep feeling much improved. She hurried about and got a fire going in the cold stove. Then she went to look in on Irene.

But Irene's bed was empty! She ran to the window and gazed at the white landscape. No one out there. Snow powder fell from the branch of a tree.

"Where is my child?" Mrs. Bobbin cried. She whipped on her coat to go out and find her.

When she pulled the door open, a wall of drift faced her. But peering over it, she could see a horse-drawn sleigh hastening up the path. And seated on the sleigh, between two large footmen, was Irene herself, asleep but smiling.

Would you like to hear the rest?

Well, there was a bearded doctor in the back of the sleigh. And the duchess had sent Irene's mother a ginger cake with white icing, some oranges and a pineapple, and spice candy of many flavors, along with a note saying how much she cherished her gown, and what a brave and loving person Irene was.

Which, of course, Mrs. Bobbin knew. Better than the duchess.

William Steig

It's not surprising that William Steig has always loved to draw. His parents and his three brothers were artists, too.

William Steig was born in 1907 in Brooklyn, New York. When he was growing up, his older brother, Irwin, gave him his first painting lessons. William also liked to read fairy tales, legends about King Arthur, and adventure stories. His favorite book was *Pinocchio*.

William Steig has written and illustrated dozens of books for young readers. Most of his books are about animal characters, but some, like *Brave Irene*, are about children. He says, "For some reason I've never felt grown up."

RESPONSE

Good Wind, Bad Wind

We know that wind is air moving over the Earth. We also know that the wind can help us or hurt us. Work with a group to make a chart. Show ways wind can help people and ways it can hurt people.

Fun with Words

The author of "Brave Irene" uses words that help you see, feel, and hear what is happening in the story. For example, he says that the duchess was like "a bright star in the sky." Write three sentences that describe how something looks, feels, and sounds. Your sentences can be silly or serious.

CORNER

Get Well Soon

The duchess was sorry to hear that Irene's mother was ill. Make a get-well card from the duchess to Mrs. Bobbin. In your card, tell Mrs. Bobbin what she should do for her fever. (You can find tips in the story.) Draw a picture on your card that will cheer up Mrs. Bobbin.

What Do You Think?

- How does Irene's mother feel at the end of the story? Why?

- Did you predict that Irene would make it to the palace? Why or why not?

- Was it a good idea for Irene to try to get to the palace by herself? Explain your answer.

Notable
Trade Book
in
Social Studies

MARY STOLZ

Storm in the Night

illustrated by PAT CUMMINGS

Storm in the night.
Thunder like mountains blowing up.
Lightning licking the navy-blue sky.
Rain streaming down the windows,
babbling in the downspouts.
And Grandfather? . . . And Thomas? . . .
And Ringo, the cat?
They were in the dark.
Except for Ringo's shining mandarin eyes
and the carrot-colored flames in the wood
stove, they were quite in the dark.
"We can't read," said Grandfather.
"We can't look at TV," said Thomas.
"Too early to go to bed," said
Grandfather.
Thomas sighed. "What will we do?"
"No help for it," said Grandfather, "I shall
have to tell you a tale of when I was a
boy."
Thomas smiled in the shadows.
It was not easy to believe that Grand-
father had once been a boy, but Thomas
believed it.
Because Grandfather said so, Thomas
believed that long, long ago, probably at
the beginning of the world, his grandfather
had been a boy.

*A*s Thomas was a boy now, and always would be.

A grandfather could be a boy, if he went back in his memory far enough; but a boy could not be a grandfather.

Ringo could not grow up to be a kangaroo, and a boy could not grow up to be an old man.

And that, said Thomas to himself, is that. Grandfather was big and bearded.

Thomas had a chin as smooth as a peach. Grandfather had a voice like a tuba.

Thomas's voice was like a penny whistle.

"I'm thinking," said Thomas.

"Ah," said Grandfather.

"I'm trying to think what you were like when you were my age."

"That's what I was like," said Grandfather.

"What?"

"Like someone your age."

"Did you look like me?"

"Very much like you."

"But you didn't have a beard."

"Not a sign of one."

"You were short, probably."

"Short, certainly."

"And your voice. It was like mine?"

"Exactly."

Thomas sighed. He just could not imagine it. He stopped trying.

He tried instead to decide whether to ask for a new story or an old one.

138

Grandfather knew more stories than a book full of stories.

Thomas hadn't heard all of them yet, because he kept asking for repeats.

As he thought about what to ask for, he listened to the sounds of the dark. Grandfather listened too.

In the house a door creaked. A faucet leaked.

Ringo scratched on his post, then on Grandfather's chair.

He scratched behind his ear, and they could hear even that.

In the stove the flames made a fluttering noise.

"That's funny," said Thomas. "I can hear better in the dark than I can when the lights are on."

"No doubt because you are just listening," said his grandfather, "and not trying to see and hear at the same time."

That made sense to Thomas, and he went on listening for sounds in the dark.

*T*here were the clocks.

The chiming clock on the mantel struck the hour of eight.

Ping, ping, ping, ping, ping, ping, ping, ping-a-ling.

The kitchen clock, very excited.

Ticktickticktickticktickety.

There were outside sounds for the listening, too.

The bells in the Congregational church rang through the rain.

Bong, bong, bong, bong, bong, bong, bong, BONG!

Automobile tires swished on the rain-wet streets.

Horns honked and hollered.

A siren whined in the distance.

"Grandfather," said Thomas, "were there automobiles when you were a boy?"

"Were there *automobiles*!" Grandfather shouted. "How old do you think I am?"

"Well . . ." said Thomas.

"Next thing, you'll be asking if there was electricity when I was your age."

"Oh, Grandfather!" said Thomas, laughing.

After a while he said, "Was there?"

"Let's go out on the porch," said Grandfather. "There's too much silliness in here."

By the light of the lightning they made their way to the front door and out on the porch.

Ringo, who always followed Thomas, followed him and jumped to the railing.

The rain, driving hard against the back of the house, was scarcely sprinkling here.

But it whooped windily through the great beech tree on the lawn, brandishing branches, tearing off twigs.

It drenched the bushes, splashed in the birdbath, clattered on the tin roof like a million tacks.

Grandfather and Thomas sat on the swing, creaking back and forth, back and forth, as thunder boomed and lightning stabbed across the sky.

Ringo's fur rose, and he turned his head from side to side, his eyes wide and wild in the flashes that lit up the night.

The air smelled peppery and gardeny and new.

"That's funny," said Thomas. "I can smell better in the dark, too."

Thomas thought Grandfather answered, but he couldn't hear, as just then a bolt of lightning cracked into the big beech tree. It ripped off a mighty bough, which crashed to the ground.

This was too much for Ringo. He leaped onto Thomas's lap and shivered there.

"Poor boy," said Thomas. "He's frightened."

"I had a dog when I was a boy," said Grandfather. "He was so scared of storms that I had to hide under the bed with him when one came. He was afraid even to be frightened alone."

"*I'm* not afraid of *anything*," Thomas said, holding his cat close.

"Not many people can say that," said Grandfather. Then he added, "Well, I suppose anybody could *say* it."

"I'm not afraid of thunderstorms, like Ringo and your dog. What was his name?"

"Melvin."

"That's not a good name for a dog," Thomas said.

"I thought it was," Grandfather said calmly. "He was my dog."

"**I** like cats," said Thomas. "I want to own a *tiger*!"

"Not while you're living with me," said Grandfather.

"Okay," Thomas said. "Is there a story about Melvin?"

"There is. One very good one."

"Tell it," Thomas commanded. "Please, I mean."

"Well," said Grandfather, "when Melvin and I were pups together, I was just as afraid of storms as he was."

"No!" said Thomas.

"Yes," said Grandfather. "We can't all be brave as tigers."

"I guess not," Thomas agreed.

"So there we were, the two of us, hiding under beds whenever a storm came."

"Think of that . . ." said Thomas.

"That's what I'm doing," said Grandfather. "Anyway, the day came when Melvin was out on some errand of his own, and I was doing my homework, when all at once, with only a rumble of warning . . . *down* came the rain, *down* came the lightning, and all around and everywhere came the thunder."

149

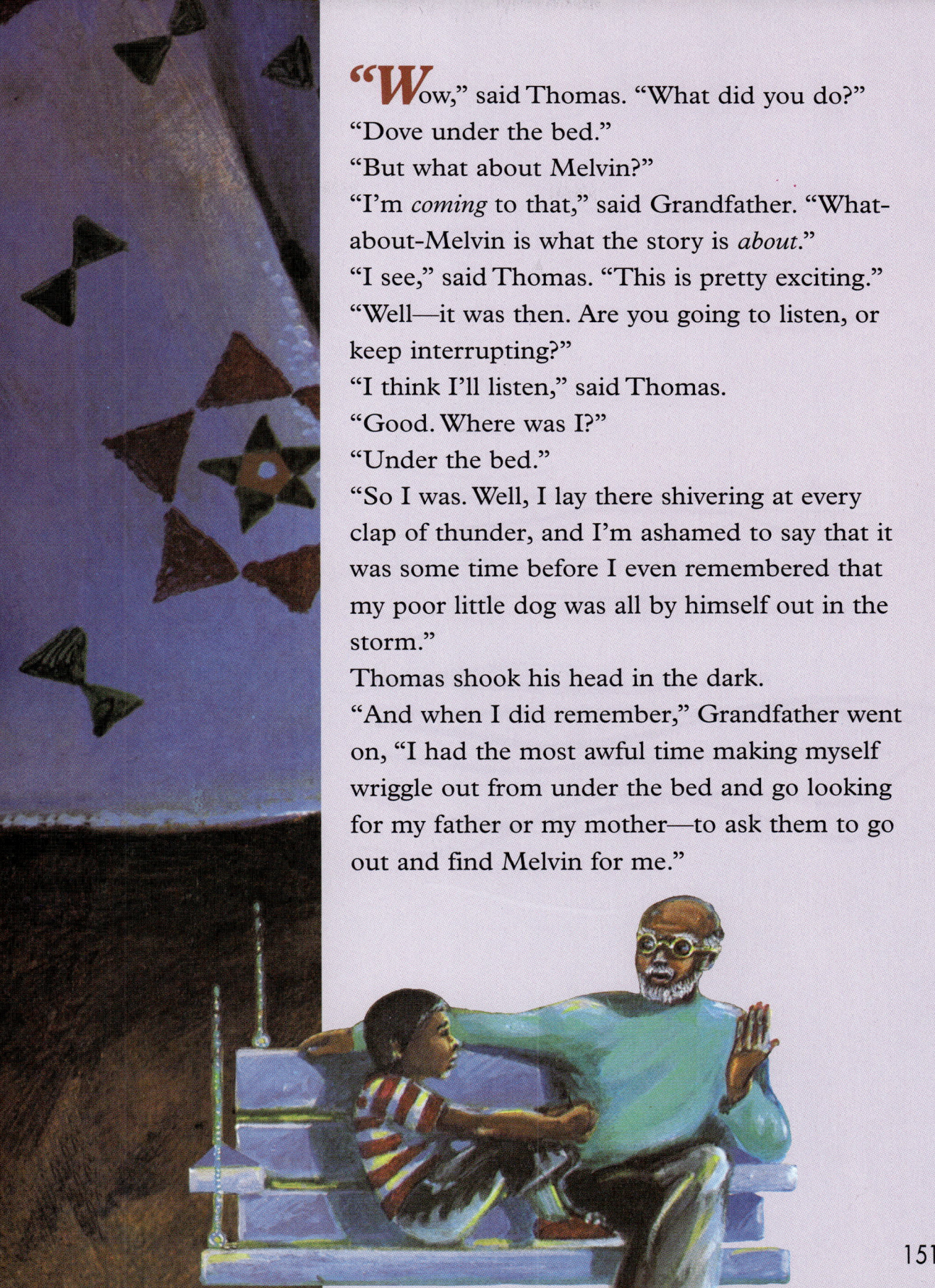

"**W**ow," said Thomas. "What did you do?"

"Dove under the bed."

"But what about Melvin?"

"I'm *coming* to that," said Grandfather. "What-about-Melvin is what the story is *about*."

"I see," said Thomas. "This is pretty exciting."

"Well—it was then. Are you going to listen, or keep interrupting?"

"I think I'll listen," said Thomas.

"Good. Where was I?"

"Under the bed."

"So I was. Well, I lay there shivering at every clap of thunder, and I'm ashamed to say that it was some time before I even remembered that my poor little dog was all by himself out in the storm."

Thomas shook his head in the dark.

"And when I did remember," Grandfather went on, "I had the most awful time making myself wriggle out from under the bed and go looking for my father or my mother—to ask them to go out and find Melvin for me."

"Grandfather!"

"I told you I was afraid. This is a true story you're hearing, so I have to tell the truth."

"Of course," said Thomas, admiring his grandfather for telling a truth like *that*. "Did you find them?"

"I did not. They had gone out someplace for an hour or so, but I'd forgotten. Thomas, fear does strange things to people . . . makes them forget everything but how afraid they are. You wouldn't know about that, of course."

Thomas stroked his cat and said nothing.

"In any case," Grandfather went on, "there I was, alone and afraid in the kitchen, and there was my poor little dog alone and afraid in the storm."

"What did you *do*?" Thomas demanded. "You didn't *leave* him out there, did you, Grandfather?"

"Thomas—I put on my raincoat and opened the kitchen door and stepped out on the back porch just as a flash of lightning shook the whole sky and a clap of thunder barreled down and a huge man *appeared* out of the darkness, holding Melvin in his arms!"

"Whew!"

"That man was seven feet tall and had a face like a crack in the ice."

"Grandfather! You said you were telling me a true story."

"It's true, because that's how he looked to me. He stood there, scowling at me, and said, 'Son, is this your dog?' and I nodded, because I was too scared to speak. 'If you don't take better care of him, you shouldn't have him at all,' said the terrible man. He pushed Melvin at me and stormed off into the dark."

"Gee," said Thomas. "That wasn't very fair. He didn't know you were frightened too. I mean, Grandfather, how old were you?"

"Just about your age."

"Well, some people my age can get pretty frightened."

"Not you, of course."

Thomas said nothing.

"Later on," Grandfather continued, "I realized that man wasn't seven feet tall, or even terrible. He was worried about the puppy, so he didn't stop to think about me."

"Well, I think he should have."

"People don't always do what they should, Thomas."

"What's the end of the story?"

"Oh, just what you'd imagine," Grandfather said carelessly. "Having overcome my fear enough to forget myself and think about Melvin, I wasn't afraid of storms anymore."

"Oh, good," said Thomas.

For a while they were silent.

The storm was spent. There were only flickers of lightning, mutterings of thunder, and a little patter of rain.

155

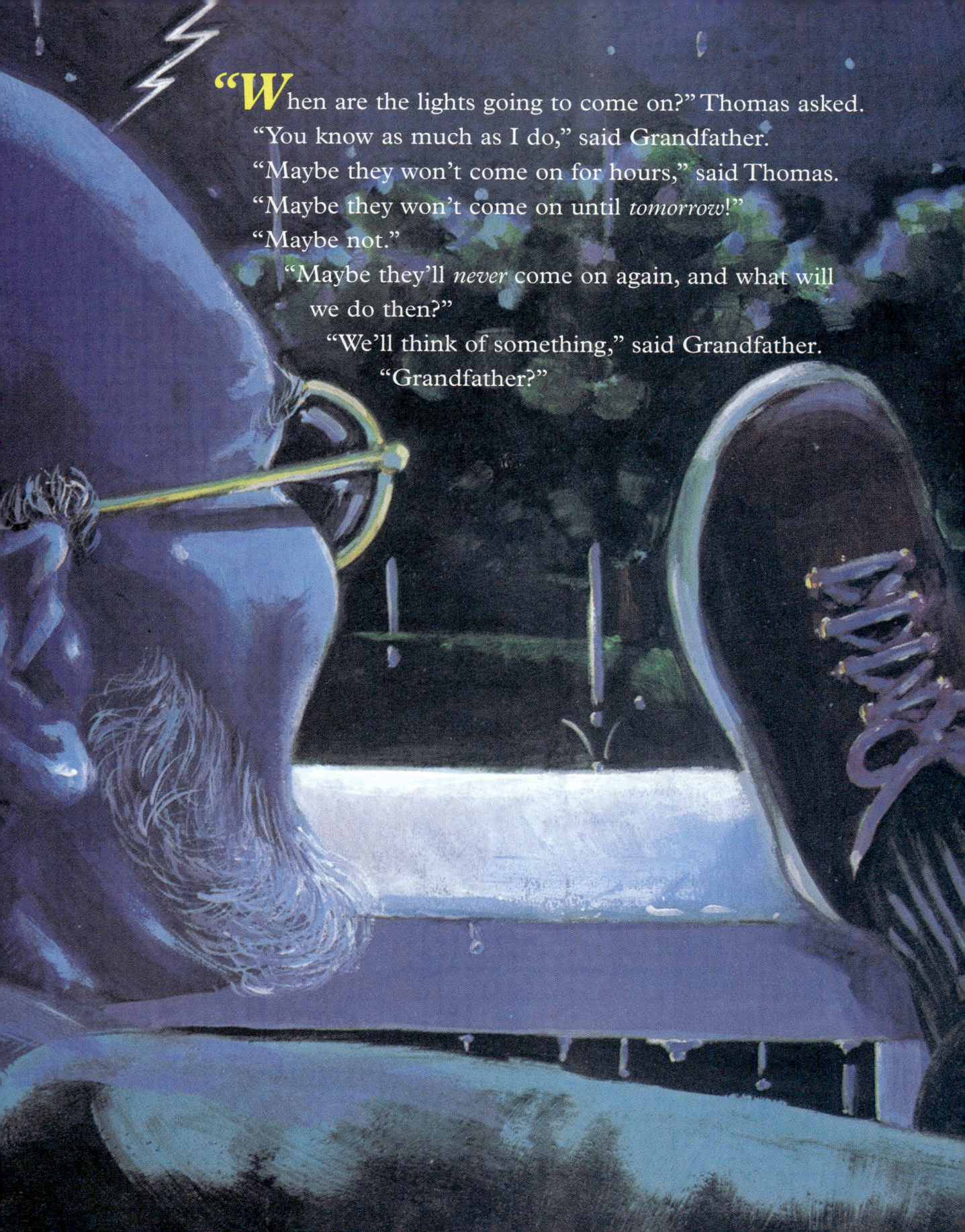

"When are the lights going to come on?" Thomas asked.

"You know as much as I do," said Grandfather.

"Maybe they won't come on for hours," said Thomas.

"Maybe they won't come on until *tomorrow*!"

"Maybe not."

"Maybe they'll *never* come on again, and what will we do then?"

"We'll think of something," said Grandfather.

"Grandfather?"

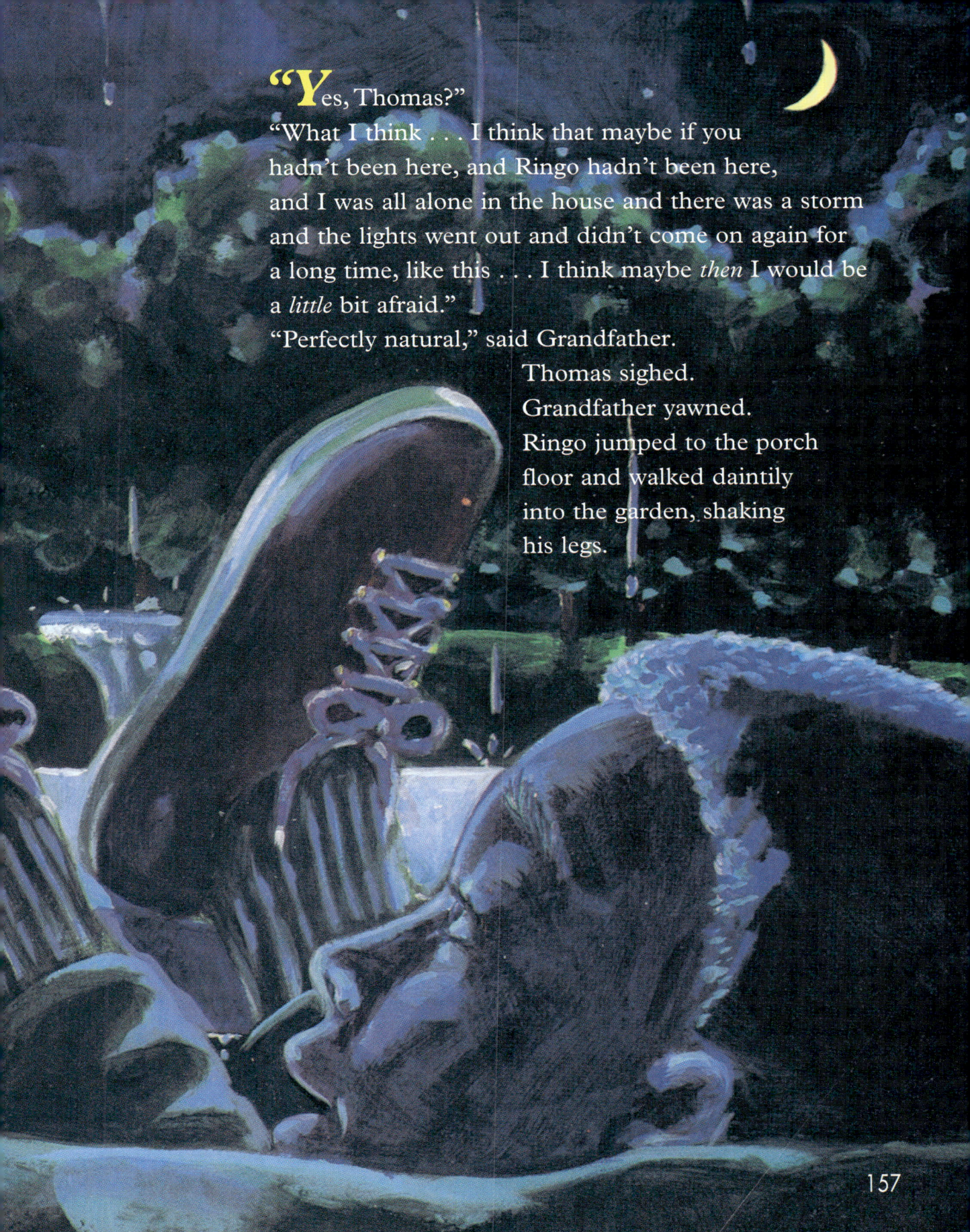

"Yes, Thomas?"

"What I think . . . I think that maybe if you hadn't been here, and Ringo hadn't been here, and I was all alone in the house and there was a storm and the lights went out and didn't come on again for a long time, like this . . . I think maybe *then* I would be a *little* bit afraid."

"Perfectly natural," said Grandfather.

Thomas sighed.
Grandfather yawned.
Ringo jumped to the porch floor and walked daintily into the garden, shaking his legs.

After a while the lights came on.
They turned them off and went to bed.

Meet Pat Cummings...

Writer Ilene Cooper spoke with Pat Cummings about the illustrations in this story.

Cooper: *Did you use models for the people in this book?*

Cummings: Yes. For Thomas, I used my cousin, Travis. I used a gentleman in my neighborhood named Theo for the grandfather, but I had to add a beard and mustache. Sometimes, I use my family, and I don't tell them they're in the book until it's finished. I've found that when I draw people I love and care about, the pictures feel much more real to me.

Cooper: *What kind of paint did you use for the art in* Storm in the Night?

Cummings: Acrylic paint—it's a kind that dries very quickly. The story has a nighttime setting, so I painted the dark background first—blacks, blues, and purples. Then I added the bright parts.

Cooper: *How old were you when you started drawing?*

Cummings: I started as soon as I could hold a pencil. I always knew I was going to be an artist when I grew up.

Travis was the model for Thomas.

This is an early sketch for the painting on pages 144 and 145.

Response Corner

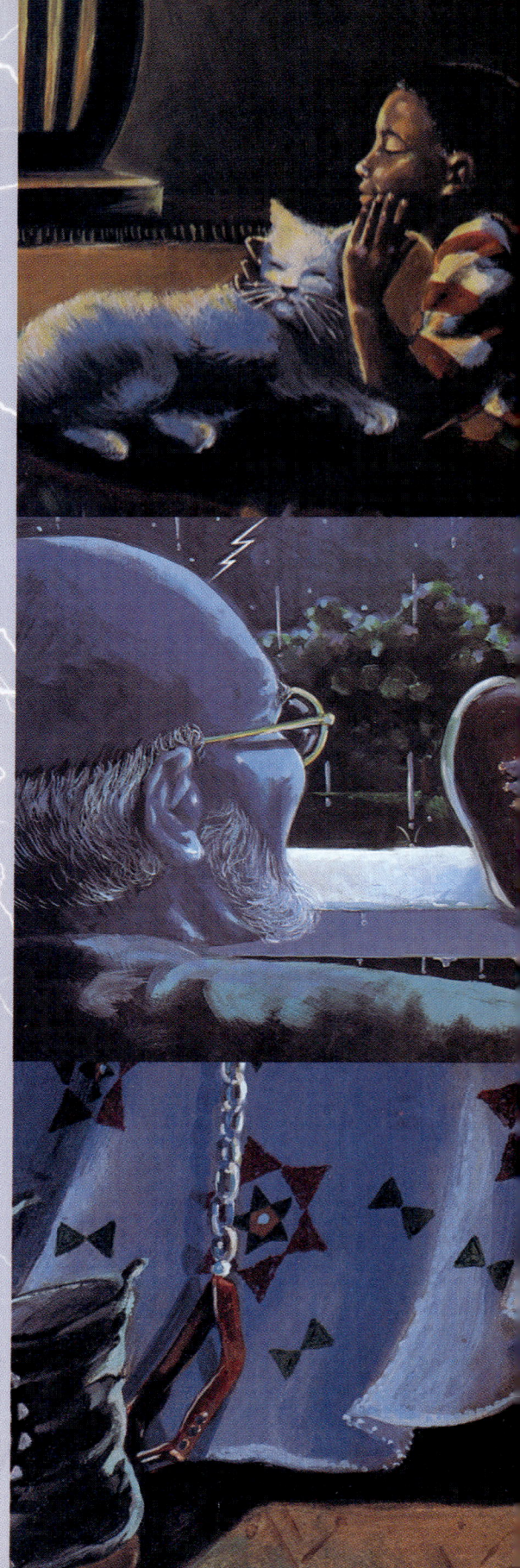

MAKE A PLAN

Where Are Your Batteries?

Suppose you had no electricity for a night. What would you do? Write a plan for an evening without electricity for you and your family. Tell how you would make dinner without electricity. What could you do for an after-dinner activity? Compare your plan with a classmate's.

WRITE A DIARY ENTRY

I'm Not Afraid...

In the beginning of the story, Thomas says that he isn't afraid of anything. Later, his grandfather teaches him an important lesson about being afraid. Write a diary entry that tells about the lesson Thomas learned.

Raining Cats and Dogs

You can get weather reports on radio and on television. You can also find them in a newspaper. Read, watch, or listen to a weather report. Then write a weather report that Thomas might have heard on the night of the storm. Describe the storm and the damage it is causing. Tell what the weather will be like for the next few days. You may want to share your weather report with your classmates.

What Do You Think?

⚡ How does Thomas feel at the end of the story? How do you know?

⚡ Do you think it's normal to be afraid of things like storms and darkness? Explain your answer.

⚡ Would Thomas and his grandfather have had such a good time if the electricity had been working? Why or why not?

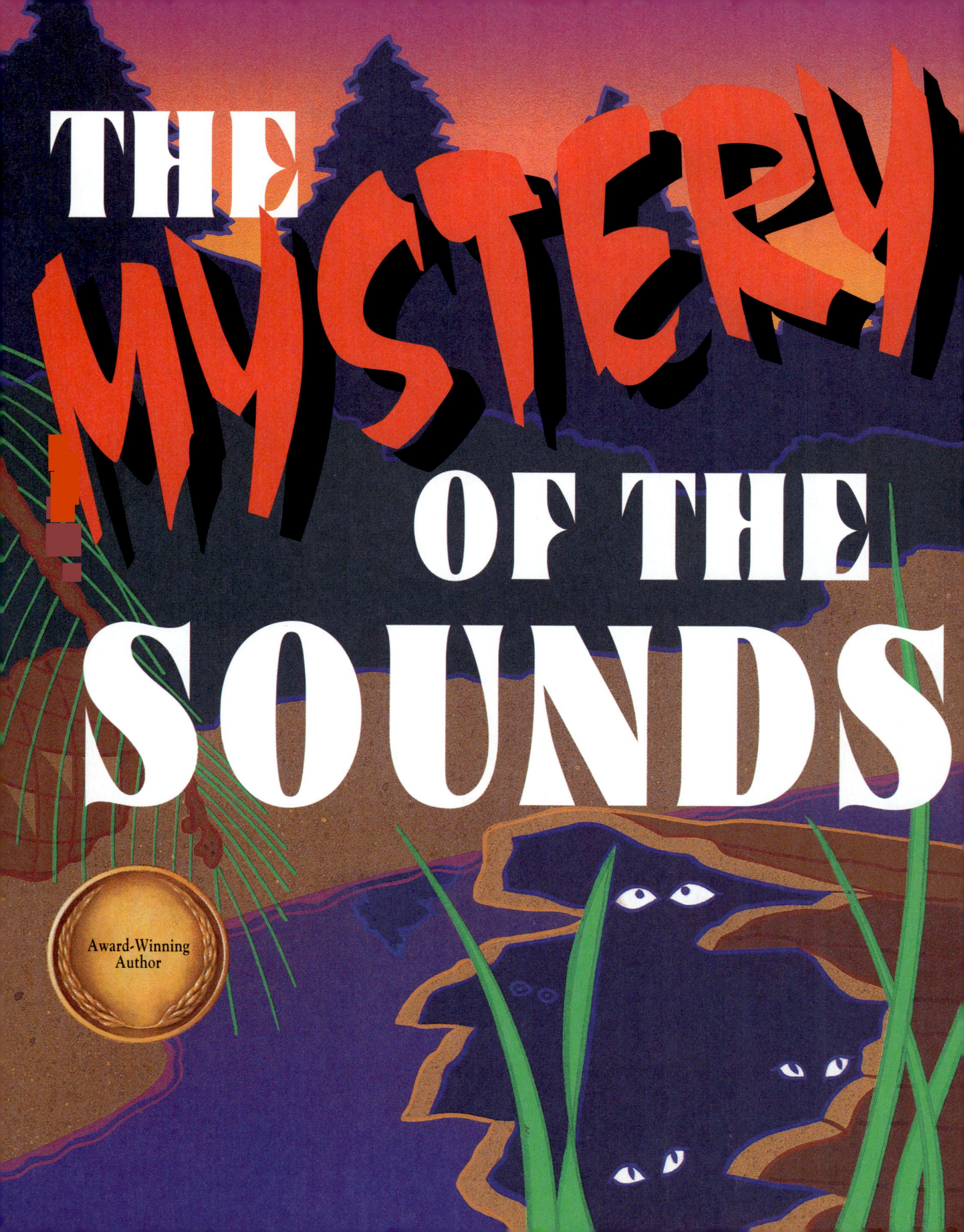

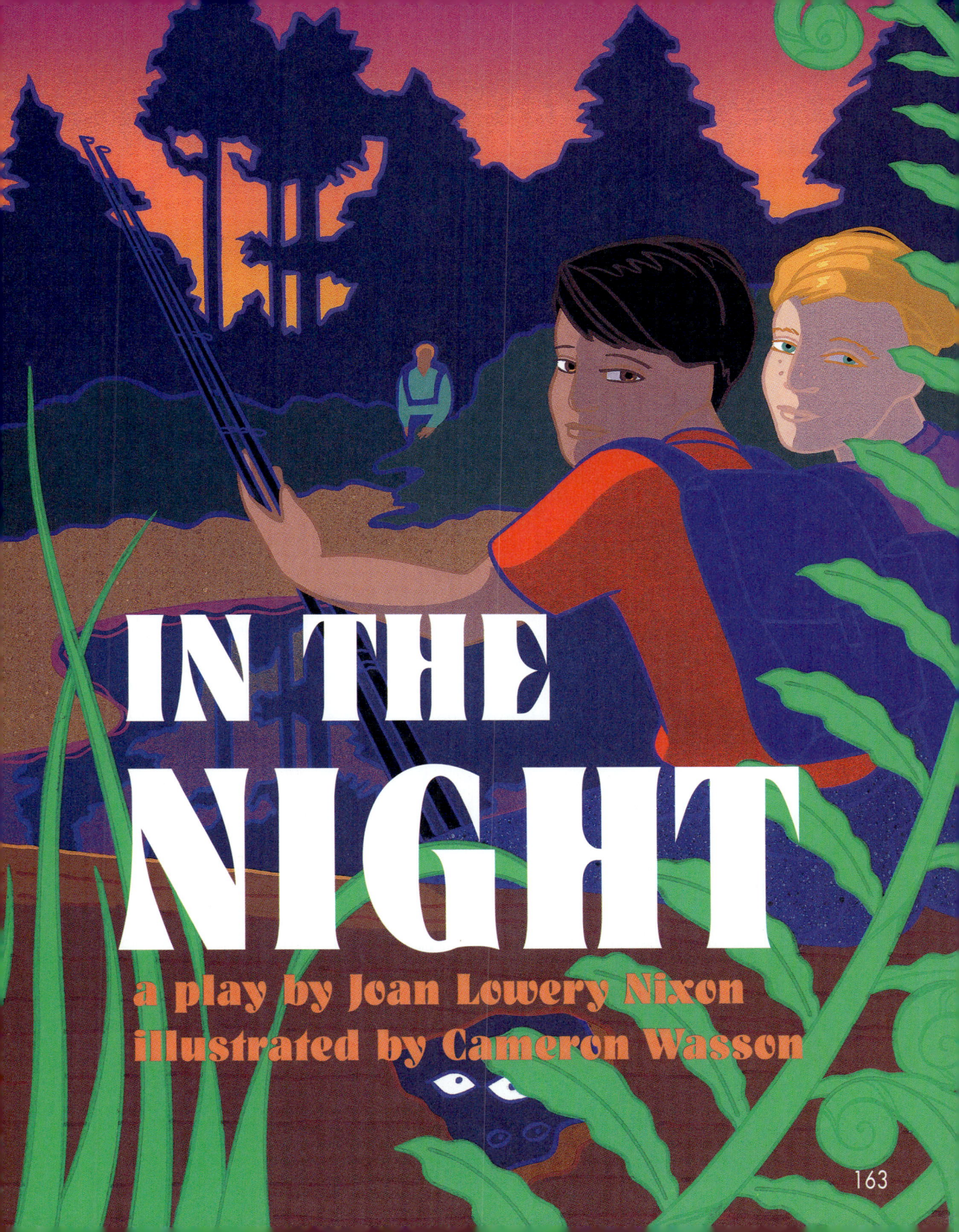

IN THE NIGHT

a play by Joan Lowery Nixon
illustrated by Cameron Wasson

CHARACTERS:

MIKE

PAUL
(his friend)

UNCLE PETE
(Mike's uncle)

TIME: *A summer evening.*

SETTING: *A clearing in the woods. On each side of stage are bushes, with twigs scattered near them. Backdrop of forest may be used.*

AT RISE: MIKE, PAUL, *and* UNCLE PETE *enter left, carrying sleeping bags.*

UNCLE PETE: Here we are, boys. This is where we'll camp for the night. It's a good thing we arrived before it got any darker.

MIKE: This is great, Uncle Pete!

UNCLE PETE (*Smiling*): Put your sleeping bags in a spot that looks comfortable. (*He puts his down at left.*)

PAUL: I can't wait to go fishing tomorrow morning! (*Looks around and puts sleeping bag down at right*)

MIKE (*Dropping sleeping bag at his feet*): I can't wait to eat dinner! When do we build the campfire?

UNCLE PETE: Right now, Mike. I'll bring the firewood,

164

and you two find some dry twigs to help get the fire started.

MIKE: Isn't this neat? (*Throws out his arms*) And the best part is that we can stay up as late as we want to!

UNCLE PETE: There's not much to do after dark. I think you'll want to go to sleep early.

MIKE (*Hopefully*): We could sit by the campfire and tell stories.

PAUL: I know an Indian story my grandfather once told me. It's about how brave young warriors used to go to the mountains to look for the Great Bear.

UNCLE PETE: That sounds like a good story, Paul. I can't wait to hear it. (UNCLE PETE *exits left.* PAUL *and* MIKE *collect twigs.*)

MIKE: Paul, this Great Bear in your story—just how big is he?

PAUL: He's supposed to be higher than a man . . . higher than the trees.

MIKE: That big, huh? (*He looks over his shoulder.*) It sure is quiet here in the woods, isn't it?

PAUL (*Standing still; listening*): It's almost too quiet. I can't hear a thing. (*Scratching, rustling sound is heard near bushes right.* PAUL *and* MIKE *freeze, look at each other.*) Except for something in the bushes. (*They stare at bushes.*)

MIKE: What do you think it is?

PAUL (*Nervously*): I don't know. (UNCLE PETE *reenters left, carrying firewood. He goes center and crouches, arranging wood.*)

UNCLE PETE: Where are the twigs, boys? (MIKE *and* PAUL *hurry to his side and hand him twigs.*)

MIKE: Uncle Pete, we heard scratching noises in the bushes.

UNCLE PETE: That doesn't surprise me. There are lots of animals in the woods. (*He "lights" fire and feeds twigs into it, then stands.*) There we are. The fire's going nicely now. I'll get the food out of the car.

PAUL and MIKE (*Ad lib*): I'll help you. Me, too. (*Etc.*)

UNCLE PETE: Thanks, anyway, but there's not that much to carry. You two stay here and keep an eye on the fire. (*He exits left. MIKE and PAUL stand very close together.*)

MIKE: I didn't think about animals being in the woods.

PAUL: Maybe they're small animals.

MIKE: *Very* small animals.

PAUL (*Holding hands close together*): Little bitty animals. (*They continue to stare at bushes. After a few moments, UNCLE PETE reenters, carrying box. He puts it down next to fire, then takes pan and ladle from box, "fills" pan, and puts it on fire.*)

UNCLE PETE: O.K., campers, you can give me a hand. Paul, why don't you stir the beans?

PAUL: Sure. (*Stirs*)

UNCLE PETE: Mike, you'll find plates and forks in the box.

MIKE: O.K., Uncle Pete.

PAUL (*Stirring*): They're beginning to bubble already.

MIKE (*Pulling plates and forks out of box*): Then let's eat!

UNCLE PETE: I'd like to hear Paul's story about the Great Bear. (*He takes ladle from PAUL and puts food onto plates. All sit at campfire, eating. UNCLE PETE is in the middle.*)

PAUL: Well, my grandfather told me that the brave young men in the tribe would go high into the mountains to see the Great Bear.

MIKE: How did they see him?

PAUL: A young man had to go into the mountains by himself. He would make a fire. He would pray to the spirits of the mountain. Then he would wait for the Great Bear.

MIKE (*Nervously*): And then what?

PAUL: If he had been a brave man, soon he would see the Great Bear. It would be higher than a man—higher than the trees.

MIKE (*Putting down plate, looking over shoulder, and moving closer to* UNCLE PETE): I don't think I'd like to see the Great Bear.

PAUL (*Putting down plate*): I wouldn't, either, especially when it's dark—the way it is now. (*He looks over his shoulder.*)

UNCLE PETE (*Putting down plate and standing*): I hope you boys aren't scaring yourselves. If you're afraid, you won't have a good time.

MIKE: Who's afraid?

PAUL: We're not afraid of anything.

UNCLE PETE: Good. (*He reaches into box, pulls out two flashlights, gives them to* MIKE *and* PAUL. *He takes out another flashlight for himself, and canteen.*) I should have thought about getting our drinking water before it got dark. I'm going down to the river to fill the canteen. You can spread out the sleeping bags, and I'll be back in a little while. (*Exits left*)

MIKE: Uncle Pete is right. If we're scared, we won't have any fun.

PAUL (*With false bravery*): I'm not scared. I'm not even thinking about the Great Bear! (*They both open sleeping bags, arrange them.*)

MIKE: I'm not scared, either! (*Rustling sound is heard from bushes right.* MIKE *jumps up, and shines his flashlight on bushes.*) What's that?

PAUL: I hope it's not the Great Bear! (*He hurries to stand beside* MIKE.)

MIKE (*Pointing*): Look at that! It's just a little raccoon.

PAUL (*Laughing shakily*): No one would be dumb enough to be afraid of a little raccoon.

MIKE (*Forcing laugh*): Yeah. No one. (*Rustling sound is heard from bushes left.* MIKE *and* PAUL *turn to face left.*) Did you hear that?

PAUL (*Shining his flashlight on bushes*): Aw, it's only a rabbit.

MIKE: Only a little kid would be afraid of a rabbit!

PAUL: Yeah. Just a scared little kid. (*There is cry from over their heads, off right. Boys grab each other.*) Look out! Use the flashlights!

MIKE (*Waving flashlight at spot high up, off right*): It's got eyes!

PAUL (*Stepping back, sighing*): All owls have eyes.

MIKE (*Nervously*): Is that what it is?

PAUL: Only a baby would be afraid of an owl.

MIKE: Yeah. Only a silly baby. (*Sound is heard from bushes right. MIKE and PAUL quickly turn flashlights right.*) What was that?

PAUL: Just a little mouse. See? (*Points*)

MIKE: Nobody would be afraid of a mouse.

PAUL: My mother would.

MIKE (*Sitting on sleeping bag*): Paul, we've been afraid of a lot of little animals that wouldn't hurt anybody.

PAUL (*Laughing nervously*): Pretty dumb of us, huh? (*Sits*)

MIKE: It's because we keep expecting the Great Bear to show up.

PAUL: I don't think the Great Bear would make a little noise. I think he'd make a big noise. (*Loudly*) Clump, clump, clump! (*Heavy footsteps are heard offstage. MIKE and PAUL jump up.*)

MIKE: Did you hear that? (UNCLE PETE *enters left. MIKE and PAUL look at each other, sigh with relief.*)

UNCLE PETE: What's the matter? You look as if you saw a ghost.

PAUL: Oh, nothing's the matter. You startled us, that's all.

UNCLE PETE: O.K., it's time to go to sleep. We want to get up very early and catch fish for breakfast. (*All take off their shoes and get into sleeping bags.*)

MIKE: It's really dark out here!

PAUL: Except for the stars. Look at them all, Mike!

UNCLE PETE: It's the Great Bear! (MIKE *and* PAUL *jump up, still in sleeping bags. They hop around.*)

MIKE: Where is it? Help!

PAUL (*Frantically*): Everybody run!

UNCLE PETE: Hey! Calm down! Look over our heads. Look at the stars. (MIKE *and* PAUL *stand still, look up. As* UNCLE PETE *talks, they slowly sit.*) The very bright groups of stars that you see are called "constellations." Every constellation has a name, and the one over our heads is called the "Big Dipper." Its Latin name is "Ursa Major," which means "Great Bear." Many people, including some Indian tribes, call it the "Great Bear."

MIKE: Paul, do you think that could be the Great Bear your grandfather told you about? Higher than a man, higher than the trees?

PAUL: Maybe it is.

MIKE (*Lying back*): And we were afraid of that?

PAUL (*Lying back*): Who was afraid? *I* wasn't.

UNCLE PETE: Go to sleep, boys. (*There is silence for a few moments, then a rumbling sound is heard.*)

PAUL (*Startled*): What's that?

MIKE (*Laughing*): I know what that sound is. It's Uncle Pete. That's the way he snores.

PAUL (*Laughing*): We're even scared of snoring! We're not really very brave, are we, Mike?

MIKE: We must be brave. We saw the Great Bear, didn't we? Just as the warriors did in your story.

PAUL: That's right. We're pretty brave, after all. (*He lies down.*) Good night, big warrior.

MIKE (*Lying back*): Good night, brave chief. (UNCLE PETE *continues to snore, as curtains close.*)

The End

A *TETON SIOUX* SONG
illustrated by John Clapp

A WOLF...

A WOLF
I CONSIDERED MYSELF,
BUT
THE OWLS ARE HOOTING
AND
THE NIGHT I FEAR.

WHEN I WAKE

Award-Winning
Poet and Illustrator

by Jonathan London
illustrated by David Diaz

When I wake in the dark

easy on the earth

and see the shape of an owl
among the stars

I lift my voice to the silence

and give thanks

to the wild night.

175

Art & Literature

What do you think Irene and Thomas would tell the boy in this picture? Would it take more courage to jump or to climb back down the ladder? Why do you think so?

The Diving Board (1947)
by Norman Rockwell

Norman Rockwell painted pictures for magazines. He became famous for his *Saturday Evening Post* covers. Rockwell's paintings show everyday life in a way that often makes people smile.

LES

LESTER'S DOG

by Karen Hesse   illustrated by Nancy Carpenter

TER'S
DOG

by Karen Hesse

illustrated by Nancy Carpenter

On long summer days, Mama scoots me out of the house after dinner. Same as always, I sit on the front stoop, watching robins rake the grass for worms, and wait for Corey to come out.

An old Chevy slides around the corner and, gears grinding, climbs up the hill. Just before the car drops down the back side of Garrison Avenue, Lester's dog tears out from under his porch and lunges at the car's wheels. You can hear him barking clear to the end of the block. He swaggers back when the car is gone and hunkers down under his porch again. I shiver, touching the scar on my nose where Lester's dog bit me when I was six.

I'm busy wishing bad things on Lester's dog when Corey comes up beside me, sticks out his hand, and pulls me off the stoop. He's tugging like he wants me to follow him up the hill, to the top of Garrison Avenue.

I shake my head. "I'm not going past Lester's dog tonight," I say. But Corey's bigger than I am, and he steers me up the hill anyway. It doesn't matter what you say to Corey, 'cause he can't hear you, and even if he could, he's too stubborn to listen.

We pass Corey's house first, and then Mr. Frank's. I sort of count on Mr. Frank always being there, sitting in his big chair, looking out over the block. Mama says he's a broken man since Mrs. Frank died, and I've been wondering for some time now just what it'd take to fix him.

I wave to him and he nods back. That's our way of talking, me and Mr. Frank.

We're almost at Lester's house now, its lawn all patched and dusty, and the grass gone from Lester's dog digging it up. I'm so scared of that dog the hair's standing up on my arms and down my spine. I try pulling Corey back the way we came, but nothing stops Corey, not even Lester's dog.

I pick up a stone and squeeze it in my fist. But even I know a little stone won't scare Lester's dog.

Corey gazes into the shadows under Lester's porch. Then he takes my hand and walks me straight past Lester's house.

I feel my heart squeezing up in my throat and my legs ready to run, but Lester's dog is too busy digging dust under his porch to notice me and Corey. Before I know it, we're past him, standing at the top of Garrison Avenue.

We look back, but Lester's dog is still under his porch, chewing dirt. I grin at Corey. "We made it," I say, swinging his hand. And Corey grins back.

We walk
down the hill
on our toes to
keep from going
too fast. At the
corner of Garrison
and Pimlico, Corey
gears up to cross the road. Traffic roars past,
whipping up licks of my shirt that are not stuck
down with sweat. I squeeze Corey's hand hard and
he frowns, his head swiveling back and forth, back
and forth, waiting for a good time to cross. And
then there's a break in the traffic, and Corey pulls
me off the curb. We fly over Pimlico Road like
Lester's dog is chasing us.

Safely on the other side, Corey pulls me toward
an old building. He stops at a wooden bulkhead.

"You brought me past Lester's dog for this?" I
ask, squinting up into Corey's face. But then I hear
something crying, and it's coming from beneath the
bulkhead door.

Corey stoops down close to the pavement. The handle to the door is broken off, so he curls his fingers around the splintery edge and lifts it over his head. I shift back and forth from one foot to the other, trying to look past Corey into the shadows of the cellar way.

Then, on the steps, I see a tiny fist of fur, knotted up. I hear it mewing, mewing like a stuck record. Corey reaches in and scoops up a single kitten. He cups it to his ear like he was listening to the sea. One skinny paw catches in the wire of Corey's hearing aid but Corey doesn't mind. He just holds that kitten to his ear, listening.

I touch Corey's shoulder, and he looks at me real serious, then eases the kitten into my hands. I feel ribs and bones jutting up under scraggly fur. The kitten wriggles and turns in my fingers. It sucks at my sweaty shirt.

Corey lowers the wooden door and motions me
to follow him back home.

"We can't take this kitten," I say. "If we take it,
we've got to care for it."

But Corey doesn't hear, and even if he does I'm
not saying anything he doesn't already know. I try
to open the bulkhead myself to put the kitten back,
but Corey stamps his foot down on the wooden door.
He takes me by my elbow, leads me to the curb, and
with his fingers clamped on to me and me
clamped on to that kitten, we tear
back across Pimlico Road.

The kitten mews and mews in my hands. I tuck
it under my shirt so it will stop shivering. Its
rough tongue scrubs the same spot on my
stomach till it drives me crazy. I slip the
kitten back out and hold it
up close to my face.

"What are we going to do with you?" I ask. "I sure can't keep you. Mama says cats make her itch." The kitten's head tips to one side like it's listening to me, and I rub its fur against my cheek.

Before I know it, we're at the top of Garrison Avenue. And there, two lawns down, is Lester's dog, staring up at us and waiting.

Corey tries taking my hand, but my hands are full of kitten. So he starts down the hill first, looking straight ahead, and I follow.

Corey gets by all right and keeps going down the hill, but Lester's dog growls at me. He growls low and nasty. My legs feel like they're dragging bricks. The kitten starts mewing and shivering worse than ever.

For a second, everything is frozen like that—
Corey almost home, and me staring at Lester's dog,
and Lester's dog staring back. And then Lester's dog
comes unstuck, and he springs at me like I was some
old Chevy.

I run, holding tight to the kitten, and Lester's dog
snaps and snarls at my heels.

I am halfway down the hill, almost to Mr.
Frank's, when I feel Lester's dog slap my back with
his paws. My head whips around, and I struggle to
stay on my feet.

Lester's dog leaps up, barking and snapping, his eyes locked on the kitten. I lift the kitten higher, but Lester's dog grabs at my shirt, ripping it with his teeth.

All the times I've been scared is all bundled into right now. But suddenly what I'm feeling is not scared. What I'm feeling is mad!

A rumbling starts deep in my throat. I glare into that dog's face, and a sound rises up from a place inside of me I didn't know was there. My whole body fills with the sound and the ground seems to shake under me as I roar at Lester's dog.

And then Lester's dog is backing off. He's leaving, whining and slinking all the way up the block, crawling on his belly to hide under Lester's porch.

All of me is trembling, and my legs feel like loose Jell-O. I sit down on the curb waiting for the shaking to pass, holding tight to the kitten.

When I look up, Corey is beside me, gazing over his shoulder toward Mr. Frank's house. But Mr. Frank isn't in his chair anymore. He's standing on the porch and he's waving. I look at Corey and I know just what to do with that kitten after all.

Walking up the swept path, I reach out to Mr. Frank.

"Here, Mr. Frank," I say, pressing the kitten into his open hands.

Mr. Frank stands by the porch rail. He doesn't call after me. He doesn't ask any questions. He just stands there talking baby talk to that scrawny kitten.

Corey lays his arm across my shoulder and I reach up and lay my arm across his. We walk down the street and settle ourselves on my stoop.

I sit with Corey like that, slapping mosquitoes and watching while cars climb up the hill past Lester's house and drop home free down the other side, till Mama calls me in.

From the Author
Karen Hesse

Lester's Dog is a story about me. I was terrified of dogs when I was a child. But I overcame my fear, just as the boy in the story does. Now I have my own dog, a big black Labrador.

Corey, the friend in the story, is based on a friend of mine. We didn't speak to each other at all because, like Corey, my friend could not hear. Even though we didn't talk, we were still good pals. He read *Lester's Dog* and told me that he loved it.

Nancy Carpenter's illustrations are the perfect match for my story. Her drawings are so alive, and I love the colors.

I've probably been writing stories since the third or fourth grade. My teachers encouraged me. At that time I was wild about Dr. Seuss books. I would go to my neighborhood library and ask when the next book would be coming out.

I like to write many kinds of stories, but in one way or another, most of them are about my own childhood!

Karen Hesse

From the Illustrator
Nancy Carpenter

Lester's Dog was one of the first stories I ever illustrated. Because I loved Karen Hesse's story, the pictures were fun to draw. I felt the story was old-fashioned, so I decided to put the characters in a 1930s setting. I used colors that seemed golden and dusty, the way we might picture a small, old-fashioned town.

I did a lot of research for *Lester's Dog.* I decided that I wanted the dog to be sharp and pointy, so I took photographs of a lot of different dogs. I put those dogs together to come up with the scary, dirty dog that belonged to Lester.

Karen Hesse told me she was delighted with my illustrations. She had planned the main character as a girl, but as soon as I read the story I drew him as a boy. We didn't meet until all of my illustrations were complete.

I would tell anyone who wants to be an illustrator to practice drawing all the time. It isn't important to draw things so that they look real. It's important to have your own style. If you practice and practice, you will find out what that style is.

RESPONSE

SIGN YOUR NAME

Corey communicates with his friend without speaking. Today, many people who cannot speak or hear use American Sign Language. Part of this language is an alphabet of hand symbols. You can find this alphabet in most encyclopedias. Use the sign language alphabet to spell your name for your classmates.

BEWARE OF DOG!

Lester's dog probably scared a lot of neighborhood kids. What should you do if you meet a dangerous dog? Write two lists. One list should tell people what to do if they meet a dog they don't know. The other list should tell dog owners how to keep their dogs from hurting people. Share your lists with your class.

CORNER

A CHEERFUL PHONE CALL

Pets can be good company for people who live alone. Show how happy Mr. Frank is about his new pet. Write what he and a good friend say on the telephone. Have them talk about Mr. Frank's feelings and about how he should care for the kitten. Then act out their telephone talk with a partner.

WHAT DO YOU THINK?

- Why does Corey make his friend walk past Lester's dog?

- How did you feel when the boy who was holding the kitten roared at Lester's dog? Why?

- Think about Mr. Frank's problem. How do you think having a kitten might help him?

from *Current Health 1 magazine*

T.HI

POSI

Tony felt discouraged. Even though he had studied hard for his last math test, he still got a bad grade. Now another big test was coming up, and he was worried that he wasn't going to do well again. Maybe, he thought, he shouldn't even bother to study.

POSITIVE!

illustrated by José Cruz

It's easy to lose your confidence at times and think that you won't do well. How you think about something, however, can affect how well you do. Scientists have studied the way our bodies and minds work together. They've found that our thoughts can affect our bodies just as our bodies can affect our thoughts.

Have you ever played a game and noticed how you try harder or run faster when your friends start to cheer for you? If you are having a good day or are in a good mood, doesn't it seem easier to do your work, try new things, or not get so upset about a problem? All these are times when you're aware of your body and mind working together.

MAKE IT HAPPEN

But you don't have to wait until you are in a good mood or have your friends cheer for you to do better. You can control how you think. When bad thoughts start to make you feel worried or discouraged, you can change them by doing things that will help you think and act more positively.

Here are some ideas:

• *Write it down.* Maybe you have a journal or diary or have tried writing down how you feel in a letter. Writing can help in a lot of ways. One is that you are able to get all those bad ideas out of your head, instead of thinking and thinking and getting upset. It's like talking to a friend about what is bothering you. You usually feel better after you do. Writing also gives you a chance to read what you wrote and think about your thoughts and feelings. Reading later, for example, about how angry you were at your sister may help you better understand how you and she felt, or help you think about ways to solve the problem. You can even choose to write it down in a letter, read it, then throw it away—instead of mailing it!

• *Talk to yourself.* Thinking is a way of talking to ourselves, and how we talk to ourselves affects how we feel. When we're in a bad mood, we say things to ourselves like "I can't do it," "It isn't fair," "I don't care." Talking to ourselves like this just makes our bad feelings worse. Listen and pay attention to what you

• *Imagine.* Have you ever looked forward to a trip and imagined all the wonderful things you hope will happen? It's hard not to get excited. You can do the same thing to help yourself when you're having a hard time. Imagine yourself doing well. Tony, for example, can imagine himself taking that test and breezing through the questions, or he can imagine his teacher handing him back his test with a great grade on it. Before a game, professional athletes often imagine themselves playing a perfect game. Imagining in this way gives you energy to keep trying, helps you learn better, and can make you feel like you will succeed.

say to yourself. If you catch yourself thinking negative things, try changing them to positive ones. Use other words like "I can," "I know I can do it," "I can solve the problem," "It's OK to make a mistake," "I can get help." It's like having a cheering team inside yourself to help you do better.

• *Find the solution.* It's easy sometimes to worry more about the problem than to think about a solution, but that usually only keeps you upset. If, for example, you think a lot about how badly your team played in the last game, or how awful you were in the school play, you'll feel crummy and won't know how to do better next time. It's OK to make mistakes; they tell us what we need to learn. Use them to figure out what you need to improve, and come up with a plan to do it. If you need help or some good ideas, talk to your parents, teachers, or friends.

GETTING STARTED

Once you start to think positively, it's hard to stop it. You'll start to feel better, and when you feel better, you'll do better. People around you will notice, and they'll say positive things to you that will help keep that good mood and confidence. What's more, your attitude can rub off on them. They'll like being around you

and may learn from you about how to handle hard times.

Like most new things, learning to think positively takes some practice. It may seem hard or awkward when you first start to write down your feelings or try to imagine positive situations. You may feel it won't help to talk to yourself differently or think up solutions, especially when you are having a hard time.

Don't try to change too quickly. Start slowly; pick one or two of the ideas to try. Ask your teacher or parent to help you recognize when bad thinking is getting you down or to encourage you to think positive. Talk to friends who have a good attitude, and ask them how they keep it up. Most of all, don't get discouraged. Think positive—you can learn to do it!

My Name Is María Isabel

by Alma Flor Ada
illustrated by Leslie Wu

Award-Winning Author

María Isabel Salazar López is proud of her name, because she is named for her relatives. She has two problems, though. Her teacher calls her Mary López, because there are too many other Marías in the class. Also, María does not have a part in the class's Winter Pageant, because the teacher called on Mary López when she assigned parts and María didn't respond. Every day the pageant draws closer and closer, and she knows her parents are eager to see her in the show.

Everything at school now revolved around plans for the Winter Pageant. The class was making wreaths and lanterns. The teacher explained to the class that Christmas is celebrated differently in different countries, and that many people don't celebrate Christmas at all. They talked about Santa Claus, and how he is called Saint Nicholas in some countries and Father Christmas in others. The class

217

also talked about the Jewish feast of Hanukkah that celebrates the rededication of the Temple of Jerusalem, and about the special meaning of the nine candles of the Hanukkah menorah.

The teacher had asked everyone to bring in pictures or other things having to do with the holidays. A lot of kids brought in photographs of their families by their Christmas trees. Mayra brought in pictures of New Year's Day in Santo Domingo. Michelle brought in a picture of herself sitting on Santa's lap when she was little. Gabriel brought in photos of the Three Kings' Day parade in Miami, Florida. He had been there last year, when he went to visit his Cuban grandmother. Marcos brought in a piñata shaped like a green parrot that his uncle had brought back from Mexico. Emmanuel showed everyone a photo album of his family's trip to Israel, and Esther brought in cards her grandfather had sent her from Jerusalem.

One day, Suni Paz came to the school. She sang Christmas songs from different countries and taught the class to sing a Hanukkah song, "The Candles of Hanukkah."

María Isabel went home humming softly "Hanukkah . . . Hanukkah . . . Let us celebrate." The bus trip seemed a lot shorter as the song ran through her head. It almost felt as if she had traveled to all those different countries and had celebrated all those different holidays.

María Isabel was still singing while she made dinner and set the table:

"With our menorah,
Fine potato latkes,
Our clay trumpets,
Let us celebrate."

Her voice filled the empty kitchen. María Isabel was so pleased she promised herself that she'd make a snowman the next time it snowed. And she'd get it finished before the garbage men picked up the trash and dirtied up the snow.

But after Suni Paz's visit to the school, the days seemed to drag by more and more slowly. María Isabel didn't have anything to do during rehearsals, since she didn't have a part in *Amahl*.

The teacher decided that after the play the actors would sing some holiday songs, including María Isabel's favorite about the Hanukkah candles. Since she didn't have a part, María Isabel wouldn't be asked to sing either.

It didn't seem to matter much to Tony and Jonathan, the other two kids who weren't in the play. They spent rehearsal time reading comics or whispering to each other. Neither boy spoke to María Isabel, and she was too shy to say anything to them.

The only fun she had was reading her library book. Somehow her problems seemed so small compared to Wilbur the pig's. He was in danger of becoming the holiday dinner. María Isabel felt the only difference was that the characters in books always seemed to find answers to their problems, while she couldn't figure out what to do about her own.

As she cut out bells and stars for decorations, María Isabel daydreamed about being a famous singer. Someday she would sing in front of a large audience, and her teacher would feel guilty that she had not let María Isabel sing in the Winter Pageant.

But later María Isabel thought, My teacher isn't so bad. It's all a big misunderstanding. . . . If only there was some way I could let her know. Even if I'm not a great singer someday, it doesn't matter. All I really want is to be myself and not make the teacher angry all the time. I just want to be in the play and to be called María Isabel Salazar López.

"I've asked my boss if I can leave work early the day of the school pageant," María Isabel's mother said one evening as she served the soup. "Papá is also going to leave work early. That way we'll be able to bring the rice and beans."

"And best of all, we can hear María Isabel sing," her father added.

María Isabel looked down at her soup. She had not told her parents anything. She knew they were going to be very disappointed when they saw the other kids in her class taking part in the play. She could just hear her mother asking, "Why didn't you sing? Doesn't the teacher know what a lovely voice you have?" María Isabel ate her soup in silence. What could she say?

"Don't you have anything to say, Chabelita?" asked her father. "Aren't you glad we're coming?"

"Sure, Papá, sure I am," said María Isabel, and she got up to take her empty bowl to the sink.

After helping her mother with the dishes, María Isabel went straight to her room. She put on her pajamas and got into bed. But she couldn't sleep, so she turned the light on and continued reading *Charlotte's Web*. María Isabel felt that she was caught in a sticky, troublesome spider's web of her own, and the more she tried to break loose, the more trapped she became.

When the librarian had told her that she would like the book, María Isabel had felt that they were sharing a secret. Now as she turned the pages, she thought that maybe the secret was that *everyone* has problems. She felt close to poor little Wilbur, being fattened up for Christmas dinner without even knowing it. He was a little like her parents, who were so eager to go to the pageant, not knowing what was waiting for them.

"It just isn't fair that this can't be a happy time for all of us!" María Isabel said out loud. She sighed. Then she turned off the light, snuggled under her blanket, and fell asleep trying to figure out a way to save Wilbur from becoming Christmas dinner.

Two days were left until the pageant. The morning was cloudy and gray. On the way to school, María Isabel wondered if it was going to snow. Maybe she would be able to make that snowman. But shortly after she got to school, it started to drizzle.

Since they couldn't go outside, the students spent their time rehearsing. No one made a mistake. Melchior didn't forget what he had to say to Amahl's mother.

Amahl dropped his crutch only once. Best of all, though, the shepherds remembered when they were supposed to enter, without bumping into the Three Kings.

Even Tony and Jonathan seemed interested in the play. They volunteered to help carry the manger and the shepherds' baskets on- and offstage.

Satisfied with the final rehearsal, the teacher decided there was time for one last class exercise before vacation. "It's been a couple of days since we've done some writing," she said when the students returned to class. "The new year is a time for wishes. Sometimes wishes come true; sometimes they don't. But it's important to have wishes and, most of all, to know what you really want. I'd like you all to take out some paper and write an essay titled 'My Greatest Wish.'"

María Isabel sighed and put away *Charlotte's Web*. Charlotte had just died, and María Isabel wondered what was going to happen to the sac of eggs that Wilbur had saved, and when Charlotte's babies would be born. But María Isabel would have to wait to find out. She bit down on her pencil and wrote: "My greatest wish . . ."

This shouldn't be so hard, María Isabel thought. If I finish writing early, I can probably finish my book. She started to write: "My greatest wish is to make a snowman. . . ."

María Isabel read over what she had just written, and realized that it wasn't what she really wanted. She put the paper aside, took out a new sheet, and wrote down the title again. "My greatest wish is to have a part in *Amahl*. . . ."

María Isabel stopped writing again. She thought, Would Charlotte have said that her greatest wish was to save Wilbur? Or would she have wished for something impossible, like living until the next spring and getting to know her children? The teacher just said that wishes don't always come true. If I'm going to wish for something, it should be something really worth wishing for.

María Isabel took out a third sheet of paper and wrote down the title again. This time, she didn't stop writing until she got to the bottom of the page.

My Greatest Wish

When I started to write I thought my greatest wish was to make a snowman. Then I thought my greatest wish was to have a part in the Winter Pageant. But I think my greatest wish is to be called María Isabel Salazar López. When that was my name, I felt proud of being named María like my papá's mother, and Isabel, like my grandmother Chabela. She is saving money so that I can study and not have to spend my whole life in a kitchen like her. I was Salazar like my papá and my grandpa Antonio, and López, like my grandfather Manuel. I never knew him but he could really tell stories. I know because my mother told me.

If I was called María Isabel Salazar López, I could listen better in class because it's easier to hear than Mary López. Then I could have said that I wanted a part in the play. And when the rest of the kids sing, my mother and father wouldn't have to ask me why I didn't sing, even though I like the song about the Hanukkah candles so much.

The rest of the class had already handed in their essays and were cleaning out their desks to go home when María Isabel got up. She quietly went to the front of the room and put her essay on the teacher's desk. María Isabel didn't look up at the teacher, so she didn't see the woman smiling at her. She hurried back to her desk to get her things and leave.

Holiday spirit was everywhere at school the next day. The paper wreaths and lanterns the class had made were hung up all over the room. The teacher had put the "greatest wish" essays up on the bulletin board, next to the cutouts of Santa Claus, the Three Kings, and a menorah.

All the students were restless. Marta Pérez smiled when María Isabel sat down next to her. "Look at the pretty Christmas card I got from my cousin in Santo Domingo," she said excitedly. María Isabel looked at the tropical Christmas scene, all trimmed in flowers. But she couldn't answer Marta because the teacher had started to speak.

"We're going to do one last rehearsal because there's a small change in the program."

The rest of the kids listened attentively, but María Isabel just kept looking down at her desk. After all, she had nothing to do with the pageant.

Then she heard the teacher say, "María Isabel, María Isabel Salazar López . . ." María Isabel looked up in amazement.

"Wouldn't you like to lead the song about the Hanukkah candles?" the teacher said with a wide grin. "Why don't you start by yourself, and then everyone else can join in. Go ahead and start when you're ready."

María Isabel walked nervously up to the front of the room and stood next to the teacher, who was strumming her guitar. Then she took a deep breath and began to sing her favorite holiday song.

While her mother was getting the rice and beans ready that night, Mr. Salazar called María Isabel over to him. "Since you can't wear makeup yet, Chabelita, I've brought you something else that I think you'll like." In the palm of his hand were two barrettes for her hair. They were shaped like butterflies and gleamed with tiny stones.

"Oh, Papi. They're so pretty! Thank you!" María Isabel exclaimed. She hugged her father and ran to her room to put them on.

At school the next day, María Isabel stood in the center of the stage. She was wearing her special yellow dress, a pair of new shoes, and the shining butterflies. She spoke clearly to the audience. "My name is María Isabel Salazar López. I'm going to sing a song about the Jewish feast of Hanukkah, that celebrates the rededication of the Temple in Jerusalem." The music started, and María Isabel began to sing:

The Candles of Hanukkah

One little candle,
Two little candles,
Three little candles,
Let us celebrate.
Four little candles,
Five little candles,
Six little candles,
Let us celebrate.
Hanukkah, Hanukkah,
Let us celebrate.
Seven little candles,
Eight little candles,
Nine little candles,
Let us celebrate.
Hanukkah, Hanukkah,
Let us celebrate.
With our menorah,
Fine potato latkes,
Our clay trumpets,
Let us celebrate.
With our family,
With our friends,
With our presents,
Let us celebrate.

And the butterflies in María Isabel's hair sparkled under the stage lights so much that it seemed that they might just take off and fly.

A Note from the Author
Alma Flor Ada

grandmother chose the name Almaflor for me. My family wanted it to be written as one word. Since in Spanish *Alma* means "soul," and *flor* means "flower," it is quite an unusual name.

Unfortunately, on my birth certificate, the clerk spelled the name as two words instead of one. When I started third grade, the teacher told me to spell my name as it was on my birth certificate. Even today I am sorry I listened to that teacher. I liked my special name. It was different from other children's, but it had been chosen with love for me, and it was mine.

There is a second reason I wrote this book. When I visit schools, I often hear people saying children's names wrong.

What are the reasons behind writing a book? Authors are not always sure. I think I wrote *My Name Is María Isabel* for two different reasons. One has to do with my own name. My mother's name is Alma. When I was born, my

Children are sometimes embarrassed to speak up, but they should not be. We should respect each other's names, as we should respect each other.

I wrote *My Name Is María Isabel* in Spanish first. Here is a page from the *third* draft of the book. In case you don't read Spanish, I should tell you that this is the part where María Isabel is about to sing in the winter pageant.

Notice that I made several changes to this draft, even though it wasn't a first draft. Some people think that authors just sit down and write until they're finished. That's certainly not true! The best authors I know keep making changes and corrections until their writing is the best it can be.

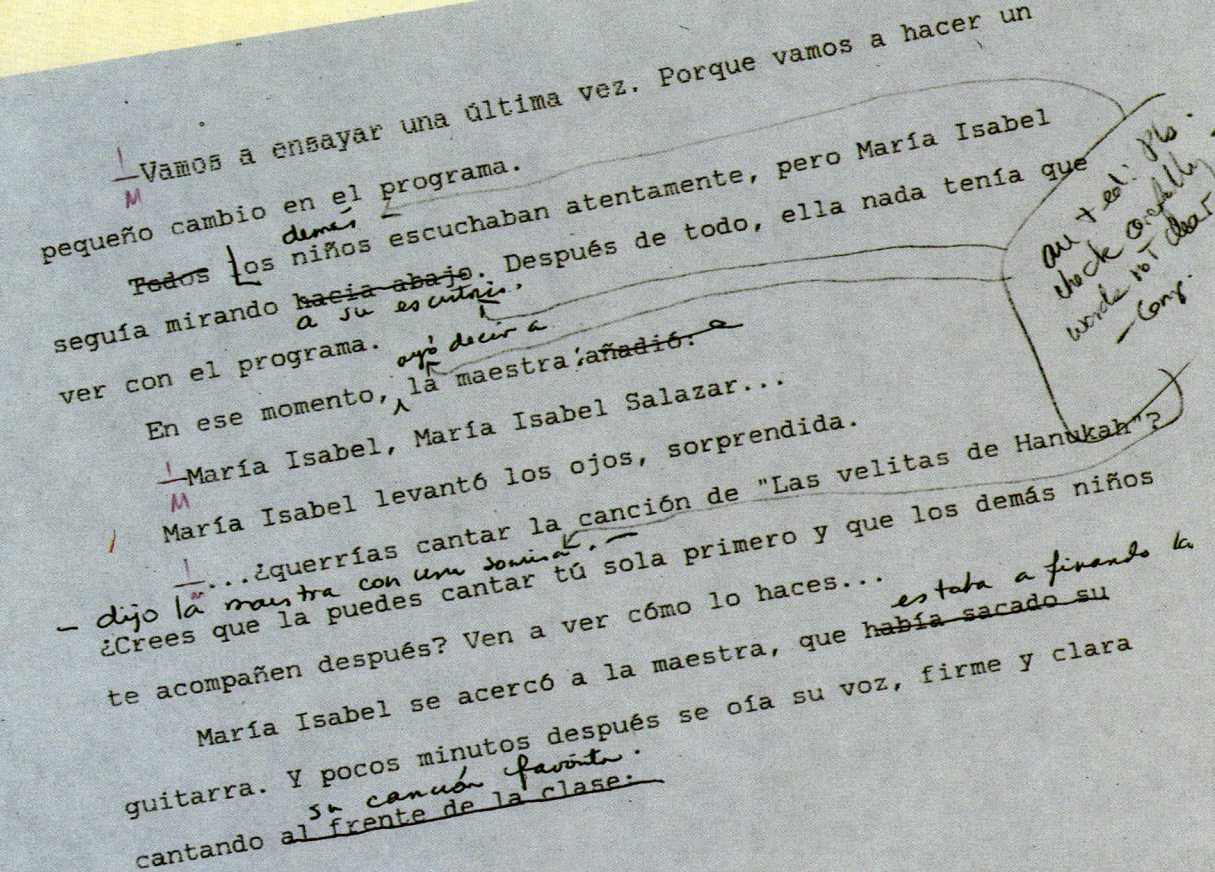

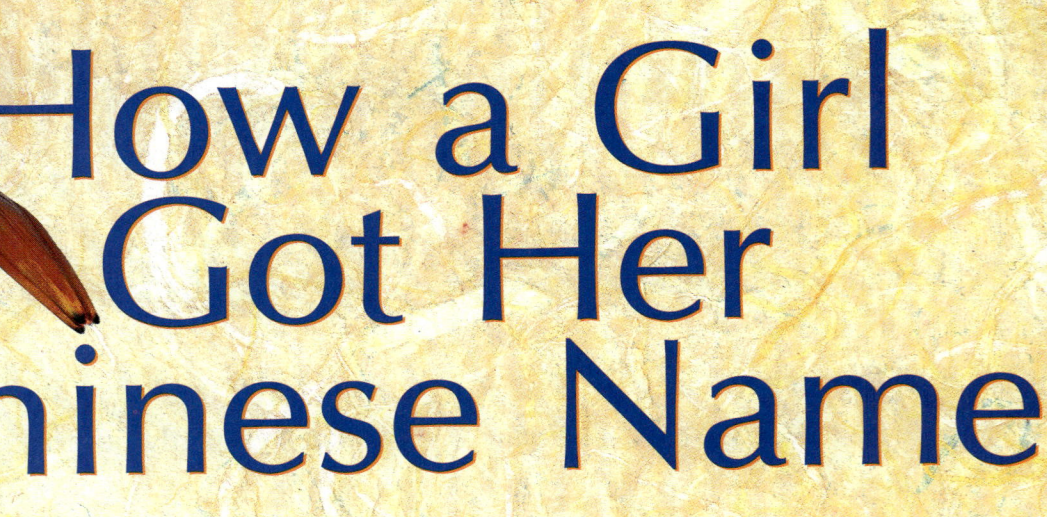

How a Girl Got Her Chinese Name

by Nellie Wong

On the first day of school the teacher asked me:
What do your parents call you at home?

I answered: Nellie.

Nellie? Nellie?
The teacher stressed the *l*'s, whinnying like a horse.
No such name in Chinese for a name like Nellie.
We shall call you *Nah Lei*[1]
which means *Where* or *Which Place.*

The teacher brushed my new name,
black on beige paper.
I practiced writing *Nah Lei*
holding the brush straight, dipping
the ink over and over.

After school I ran home.
Papa, Mama, the teacher says my name is *Nah Lei.*
I did not look my parents in the eye.

Nah Lei? Where? Which Place?
No, that will not do, my parents answered.
We shall give you a Chinese name,
we shall call you *Lai Oy*.[2]

So back to school I ran,
announcing to my teacher and friends
that my name was no longer *Nah Lei*,
not *Where*, not *Which Place*,
but *Lai Oy, Beautiful Love*,
my own Chinese name.
I giggled as I thought:
Lai Oy could also mean *lost pocket*
depending on the heart
of a conversation.

But now in Chinese school
I was *Lai Oy*, to pull out of my pocket
every day, after American school,
even Saturday mornings,
from Nellie, from *Where*, from *Which Place*
to *Lai Oy*, to *Beautiful Love*.

Between these names
I never knew I would
    ever get lost.

_____

[1] *Nah Lei*: pronounced [nä lā]
[2] *Lai Oy*: pronounced [lī oi]

Lai Oy

Who Is Special?

Everyone is special. Make a poster that tells about you. Include a photo of yourself. Then spell out your name and decorate it. You can use colored markers, yarn, glitter, or anything else. Then, from magazines, cut out pictures and words that show what you are like. Share your poster with your classmates.

Response Corner

Where Did You Get Your Name?

María Isabel Salazar López and the girl in "How a Girl Got Her Chinese Name" thought their names were special. Find out whether your family has a special naming custom. Ask your parents or grandparents. Write a list of important family names, and tell why they are important.

Holiday Treasures

The Winter Pageant showed how different holidays are celebrated around the world. Bring in a picture or another item that helps to show how you and your family celebrate a holiday. Tell a friend why the picture or other item is special.

What Do You Think?

- How does María Isabel solve her problems?

- Do you think María Isabel is brave? Explain your answer.

- It can be hard to start in a new school. What are some things you could do to help a new student in your school?

235

THEME WRAP-UP

The characters in this theme discover different kinds of courage. How do other people help them be brave? Do any of the characters help other people? How?

Which character in this theme is the bravest? Support your answer with reasons and examples.

ACTIVITY CORNER

Has anyone ever helped you to be brave? Maybe someone gave you advice, or maybe you just followed someone's example. Write a thank-you note to the person who helped you, and explain what you have learned about bravery.

THE POWER OF TEAMWORK

Do you play on a sports team? Do you "pitch in" to help your family at home? Maybe you work with your classmates sometimes. In this theme you will learn that working together is a very good way to get things done!

THE POWER OF TEAMWORK

CONTENTS

City Green
written and illustrated by
DyAnne DiSalvo-Ryan

Kids and Kicks
by Deborah H. DeFord

The New Kid
by Mike Makley

Centerfield Ballhawk
by Matt Christopher

Playing Outfield and
Prediction: School P.E.
by Isabel Joshlin Glaser

The Turnip
retold by Pleasant DeSpain

After the Last Hard Freeze
by Arnold Adoff

Art and Literature:
Detroit Industry
by Diego Rivera

Lon Po Po
translated and illustrated by
Ed Young

The Three Little Javelinas
by Susan Lowell

BOOKSHELF

RAMONA QUIMBY, AGE 8

by Beverly Cleary

Ramona works hard to help her family get through tough times.

Newbery Honor;
ALA Notable Book;
SLJ Best Books;
Children's Choice

Signatures Library

UP GOES THE SKYSCRAPER!

by Gail Gibbons

Planners, construction workers, electricians, and plumbers all work together to build a skyscraper.

Award-Winning Author and Illustrator

Signatures Library

The Story of the Three Kingdoms
by Walter Dean Myers

People can live in all regions of the Earth because they are able to communicate and to work together.

Award-Winning Author and Illustrator

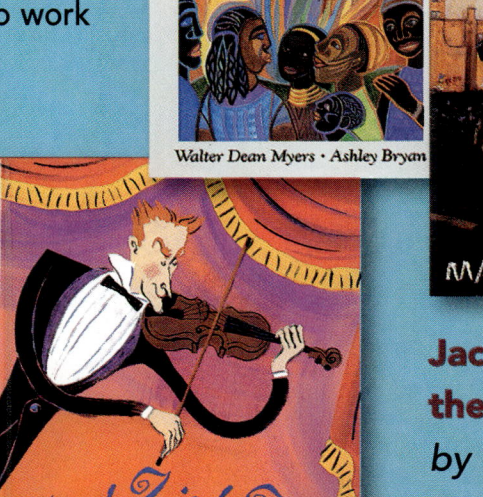

Zin! Zin! Zin! a Violin
by Lloyd Moss

All the members of an orchestra contribute to its beautiful music.

ALA Notable Book
Caldecott Honor
New York Times Best Illustrated Book

Jackson Jones and the Puddle of Thorns
by Mary Quattlebaum

Jackson works with his best friend to earn money by raising flowers.

City Green
DyAnne DiSalvo-Ryan

CITY

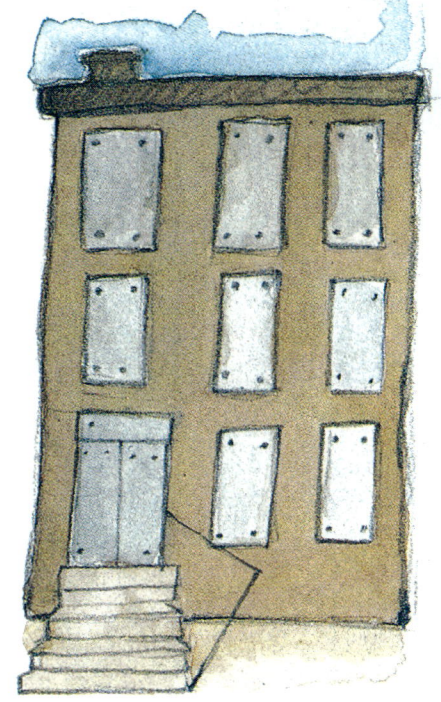

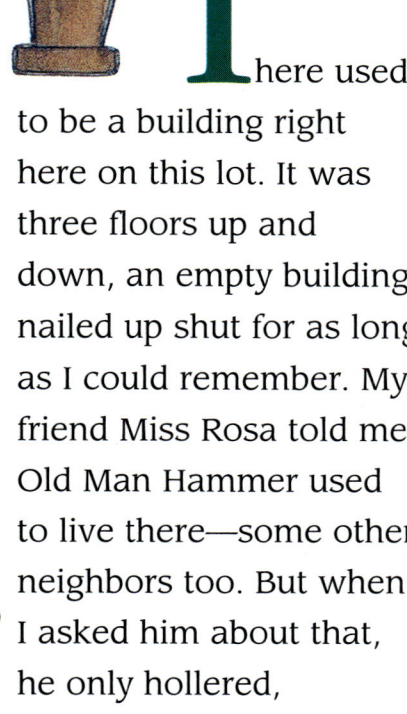

There used to be a building right here on this lot. It was three floors up and down, an empty building nailed up shut for as long as I could remember. My friend Miss Rosa told me Old Man Hammer used to live there—some other neighbors too. But when I asked him about that, he only hollered, "Scram."

Old Man Hammer, hard as nails.

GREEN

by DyAnne DiSalvo-Ryan

Last year two people from the city came by, dressed in suits and holding papers. They said, "This building is unsafe. It will have to be torn down."

By winter a crane with a wrecking ball was parked outside. Mama gathered everyone to watch from our front window. In three slow blows that building was knocked into a heap of pieces. Then workers took the rubble away in a truck and filled the hole with dirt.

Now this block looks like a big smile with one tooth missing. Old Man Hammer sits on his stoop and shakes his head. "Look at that piece of junk land on a city block," Old Man Hammer says. "Once that building could've been saved. But nobody even tried."

And every day when I pass this lot it makes me sad to see it. Every single day.

Then spring comes, and right on schedule Miss Rosa starts cleaning her coffee cans. Miss Rosa and I keep coffee cans outside our windowsills. Every year we buy two packets of seeds at the hardware store—sometimes marigolds, sometimes zinnias, and one time we tried tomatoes. We go to the park, scoop some dirt, and fill up the cans halfway.

This time Old Man Hammer stops us on the way to the park. "This good for nothin' lot has plenty of dirt right here," he says.

Then all at once I look at Miss Rosa. And she is smiling back at me. "A *lot* of dirt," Miss Rosa says.

"Like one big coffee can," I say.

That's when we decide to do something about this lot.

Quick as a wink I'm digging away, already thinking of gardens and flowers. But Old Man Hammer shakes his finger. "You can't dig more dirt than that. This lot is city property."

Miss Rosa and I go to see Mr. Bennett. He used to work for the city. "I seem to remember a program," he says, "that lets people rent empty lots."

That's how Miss Rosa and I form a group of people from our block. We pass around a petition that says: WE WANT TO LEASE THIS LOT. In less than a week we have plenty of names.

"Sign with us?" I ask Old Man Hammer.

"I'm not signin' nothin'," he says. "And nothin' is what's gonna happen."

But something did.

The next week, a bunch of us take a bus to city hall. We walk up the steps to the proper office and hand the woman our list. She checks her files and types some notes and makes some copies. "That will be one dollar, please."

We rent the lot from the city that day. It was just as simple as that.

Saturday morning I'm up with the sun and looking at this lot. My mama looks out too. "Marcy," she says, and hugs me close. "Today I'm helping you and Rosa."

After shopping, Mama empties her grocery bags and folds them flat to carry under her arm. "Come on, Mrs. B.," Mama tells her friend. "We're going to clear this lot."

Then what do you know but my brother comes along. My brother is tall and strong. At first, he scratches his neck and shakes his head just like Old Man Hammer. But Mama smiles and says, "None of that here!" So all day long he piles junk in those bags and carries them to the curb.

Now, this time of day is early. Neighbors pass by and see what we're doing. Most say, "We want to help too." They have a little time to spare. Then this one calls that one and that one calls another.

"Come on and help," I call to Old Man Hammer.

"I'm not helpin' nobody," he hollers. "You're all wastin' your time."

Sour grapes my mama'd say, and sour grapes is right.

Just before supper, when we are good and hungry, my mama looks around this lot. "Marcy," she says, "you're making something happen here."

Next day the city drops off tools like rakes and brooms, and a Dumpster for trash. Now there's even more neighbors to help. Miss Rosa, my brother, and I say "Good morning" to Old Man Hammer, but Old Man Hammer just waves like he's swatting a fly.

"Why is Old Man Hammer so mean and cranky these days?" my brother asks.

"Maybe he's really sad," I tell him. "Maybe he misses his building."

"That rotten old building?" My brother shrugs. "He should be happy the city tore down that mess."

"Give him time," Miss Rosa says. "Good things take time."

Mr. Bennett brings wood—old slats he's saved—and nails in a cup. "I knew all along I saved them for something," he says. "This wood's good wood."

Then Mr. Rocco from two houses down comes, carrying two cans of paint. "I'll never use these," he says. "The color's too bright. But here, this lot could use some brightening up."

Well, anyone can tell with all the excitement that something is going on. And everyone has an idea about what to plant—strawberries, carrots, lettuce, and more. Tulips and daisies, petunias, and more! Sonny turns the dirt over with a snow shovel. Even Leslie's baby tries to dig with a spoon.

For lunch, Miss Rosa brings milk and jelly and bread and spreads a beach towel where the junk is cleared. By the end of the day a fence is built and painted as bright as the sun.

Later, Mama kisses my cheek and closes my bedroom door. By the streetlights I see Old Man Hammer come down his steps to open the gate and walk to the back of this lot. He bends down quick, sprinkling something from his pocket and covering it over with dirt.

In the morning I tell my brother. "Oh, Marcy," he says. "You're dreaming. You're wishing too hard."

But I know what I saw, and I tell my mama, "Old Man Hammer's planted some seeds."

Right after breakfast, I walk to the back of this lot. And there it is—a tiny raised bed of soil. It is neat and tidy, just like the rows we've planted. Now I know for sure that Old Man Hammer planted something. So I pat the soil for good luck and make a little fence to keep the seeds safe.

Every day I go for a look inside our garden lot. Other neighbors stop in too. One day Mrs. Wells comes by. "This is right where my grandmother's bedroom used to be," she says. "That's why I planted my flowers there."

I feel sad when I hear that. With all the digging and planting and weeding and watering, I'd forgotten about the building that had been on this lot. Old Man Hammer had lived there too. I go to the back, where he planted his seeds. I wonder if this was the place where his room used to be.

I look down. Beside my feet, some tiny stems are sprouting. Old Man Hammer's seeds have grown! I run to his stoop. "Come with me!" I beg, tugging at his hand. "You'll want to see."

I walk him past the hollyhocks, the daisies, the peppers, the rows of lettuce. I show him the strawberries that I planted. When Old Man Hammer sees his little garden bed, his sour grapes turn sweet. "Marcy, child." He shakes his head. "This lot was good for nothin'. Now it's nothin' but good," he says.

Soon summertime comes, and this lot really grows. It fills with vegetables, herbs, and flowers. And way in the back, taller than anything else, is a beautiful patch of yellow sunflowers. Old Man Hammer comes every day. He sits in the sun, eats his lunch, and sometimes comes back with supper.

Nobody knows how the sunflowers came—not Leslie, my brother, or Miss Rosa. Not Mr. Bennett, or Sonny, or anyone else. But Old Man Hammer just sits there smiling at me. We know whose flowers they are.

Talking to DyAnne DiSalvo-Ryan

Writer Ilene Cooper talked to DyAnne DiSalvo-Ryan to find out about her work and her childhood.

Ilene Cooper: *You're a real city kid, aren't you?*

DyAnne DiSalvo-Ryan: *I sure am. I grew up in the Park Slope section of Brooklyn, New York.*

Cooper: *Is Brooklyn the setting for City Green?*

DiSalvo-Ryan: *Yes. The idea came straight from the streets of Brooklyn. I used to volunteer at a soup kitchen. Every day I walked past a beautiful city garden that was in the middle of the block. City Green is like that garden.*

Cooper: *What about the characters in the book, like Old Man Hammer? Are your characters based on real people?*

DiSalvo-Ryan: (laughing) *There's always been an "Old Man Hammer" in my life. I remember as a child having grouchy neighbors. Of course, I can be a little grouchy, too. The rest of the characters in the book are a mix of fact and fiction.*

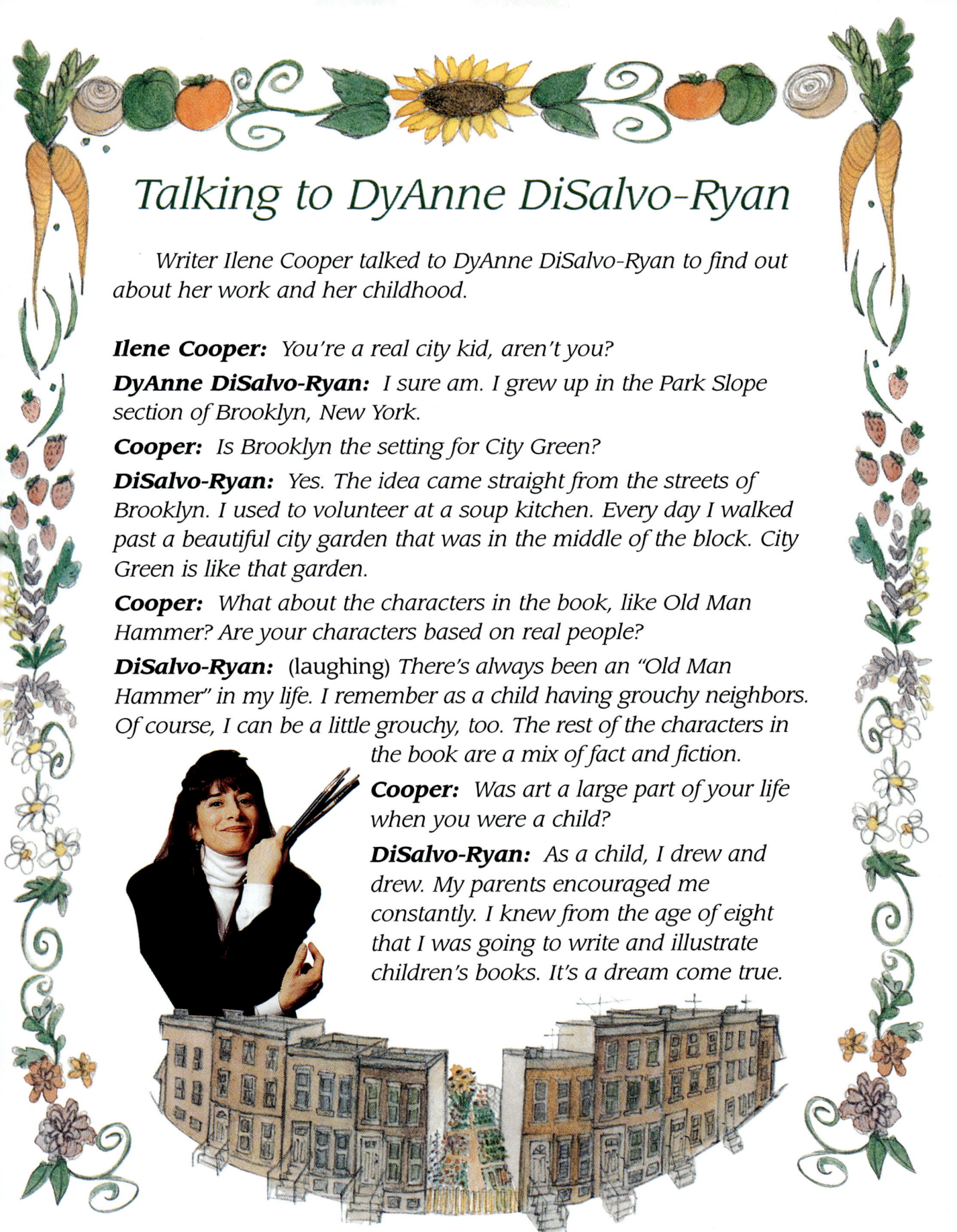

Cooper: *Was art a large part of your life when you were a child?*

DiSalvo-Ryan: *As a child, I drew and drew. My parents encouraged me constantly. I knew from the age of eight that I was going to write and illustrate children's books. It's a dream come true.*

Response Corner

Let's Make a Difference

With your classmates, walk around your classroom and find places that could look better than they do. Together, list ways you could fix them up. Choose one or two things on your list, and make plans to do them soon.

Sing a Happy Tune!

Old Man Hammer is so happy among his beautiful sunflowers that he may feel like singing! Write a song that tells how he feels about the garden. Use the music from a song you know. You may want to copy the words of your song and ask your classmates to sing along with you.

Do Something!

No one tried to save the building
Old Man Hammer lived in. Find
a place in your community that
might need saving. What would
you need to do to save it? Who
would you write to, and what
would you say? Write a letter to a
person who could help you save
that part of your community.

What Do You Think?

● What does Marcy know about
Old Man Hammer that other
people do not know?

● What kind of person is Marcy?
Explain your answer.

● What did you learn about
working together from reading
this story?

257

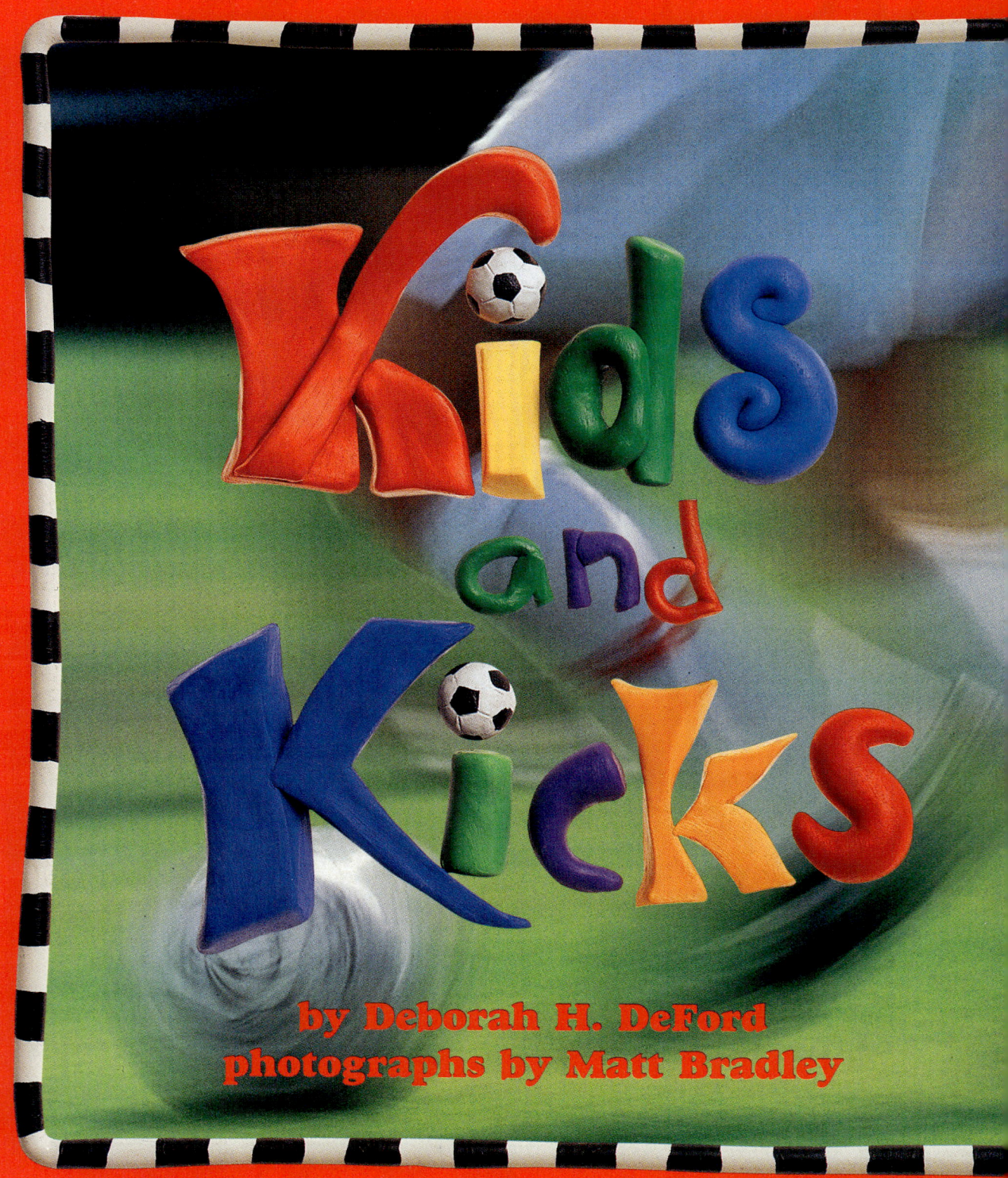

Kids and Kicks

by Deborah H. DeFord
photographs by Matt Bradley

A gray-shirted player runs down the soccer field. She taps the ball along the ground in front of her with her feet. A blue-shirted player darts in front of her. But the gray-shirted player quickly boots the ball to her teammate beside her. The teammate zooms toward the goal. He gives the ball a quick side kick toward the net. The goalkeeper dives for the ball, her arms stretched out. But she's too late. The ball flies past. The gray team has scored!

Every year, thousands of kids all over the U.S. share exciting moments just like this. How did these kids get started in soccer?

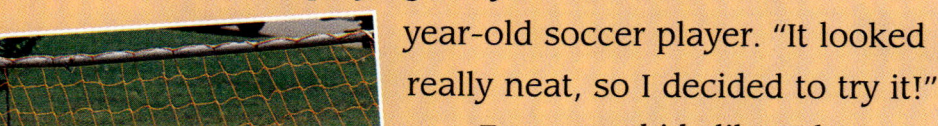

"I watched older kids playing," says Ethan, one nine-year-old soccer player. "It looked really neat, so I decided to try it!"

For many kids like Ethan, trying is the first step to a lot of fun. Soccer is becoming the favorite sport of more and more U.S. kids.

◀ **Heads up, everyone! The blue team is close to their goal.**

 What's so GREAT about SOCCER?

"You learn to do things with the ball that you never expected to do," explains Steven, another young soccer player. Through practice and games, kids learn how to handle the ball with their feet, legs, bodies, and heads. And they learn how *never* to use their hands or arms.

Kids also learn how to play as team members.

"You have friends to pass the ball to," says Ethan. "That's great, because the game doesn't depend just on you."

Lots of kids like soccer because any kid can play. There are eleven field positions on each team. Each position calls for different skills. There are places for kids of any shape and size.

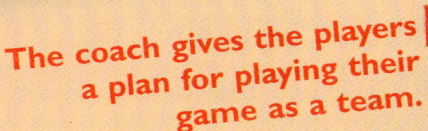
The coach gives the players a plan for playing their game as a team.

During game time, the action almost never stops. So every player spends some time on the field. When not on the field, players rest on the bench, cheering for their teammates.

"On the field," Ethan says, "I'm not cheering at good plays. And I'm not feeling bad when we don't do well. I have my mind set on the game."

Soccer teaches kids to work hard, enjoy winning, and lose as good sports.

And what makes a good team? Steven and Ethan agree: "A good team is players doing their best at what they are supposed to do!" ❖

The game is over. Every player has done his or her best. But more important, the players have done their best TOGETHER!

THE NEW KID

by Mike Makley
illustrated by Steve Cieslawski

Our baseball team never did very much,
we had me and PeeWee and Earl and Dutch.
And the Oak Street Tigers always got beat
until the new kid moved in on our street.

The kid moved in with a mitt and a bat
and an official New York Yankee hat.
The new kid plays shortstop or second base
and can outrun us all in any place.

The kid never muffs a grounder or fly
no matter how hard it's hit or how high.
And the new kid always acts quite polite,
never yelling or spitting or starting a fight.

We were playing the league champs just last week;
they were trying to break our winning streak.
In the last inning the score was one-one,
when the new kid swung and hit a home run.

A few of the kids and their parents say
they don't believe that the new kid should play.
But she's good as me, Dutch, PeeWee, or Earl,
so we don't care that the new kid's a girl.

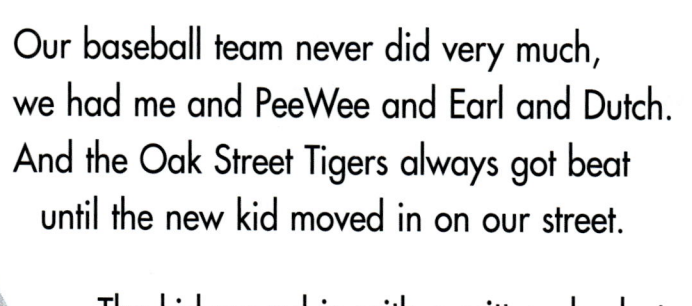

CENTERFIELD

by Matt Christopher

Award-Winning Author

José Mendez is the best fielder on his team. He makes catches that his teammates only dream about. But José doesn't realize how good he is at fielding. He is too busy trying to become a better batter. He thinks he has to be as good as or better than his father, who batted .375 in the minor leagues.

BALLHAWK

illustrated by Lisa Pomerantz

MUDDERS

"*S*teeerike!" yelled the ump.

Then, "Steeerike two!"

"Belt it, José!" cried the coach.

José's heart pounded like crazy. This was it.

Crack! His bat met the ball head-on. The white sphere took off like a rocket for left field and sailed over the fence for a home run!

The Mudders' fans screamed their heads off. "All right, José!" they shouted as he dropped his bat and trotted around the bases.

Bus singled that inning, too, but the Mudders failed to score him. Mudders 5, Bulls 2.

The Stockade Bulls came to bat blowing through their nostrils. After two outs and a man on third base, Adzie Healy lambasted one. It had a home run label on it as it zoomed toward the center field fence. José started to run back the instant he had seen it hit.

He was almost up against the fence when the ball came flying down over his head. He jumped—and caught it!

"**Y**es! Great catch, man!" Barry yelled. "Saved us a run!"

José smiled and tossed the ball to him as they ran in together. "Just lucky," he said.

"Sure." Barry laughed.

Alfie singled, and Turtleneck walked, bringing José up to the plate. *I've got to get a hit*, he thought. *I've got to, or I'm sunk.*

He grounded out.

Good thing Dad isn't at the game, he thought as he returned to the bench. At least he's got Carmen.

The Mudders kept the Bulls from scoring in the bottom of the fourth, then went to town at their turn at bat, scoring two runs. Mudders 7, Bulls 2.

MUDDERS 7
BULLS 2

In the bottom of the fifth, the Stockade Bulls showed the real power they had, as if they had purposely kept it hidden until now. They pounded Sparrow for five runs, tying up the score, 7 to 7.

MUDDERS 7
BULLS 7

In the top of the sixth, Barry singled, then Turtleneck flied out. José slowly stepped to the plate. This could be it, he thought. A hit now could break the tie. And it would mean a .500 average for him.

He flied out.

José's heart sank into his stomach. He wished he could vanish.

Then T.V. struck out, and the Bulls were back up to the plate.

The first two guys got on. Then Ted Jackson popped up to the pitcher, and Adzie blasted a line drive to center field. It looked as if it were going to hit the ground halfway between second base and José.

José was after it like a gazelle. He knew he had to catch that ball or the game was over.

He dove, then felt the solid *thud!* as the ball landed squarely in his glove.

The crowd stood up, and clapped and cheered for a full minute.

On the next play, a grounder skittered through T.V.'s legs. A run scored, and the game was over. The Stockade Bulls beat the Peach Street Mudders, 8 to 7.

"It's my fault we lost! My fault!" T.V. moaned as José caught up with him and they walked off the field together.

"Don't sweat it, man!" José said. "It's not the end of the world! Who's perfect?"

He was thinking of his batting as he said it. One out of four was .250. Far, far from a .375 average. His father would never, *never* think much of him as a baseball player.

Suddenly he heard his name called. "José! Wait up!" He turned.

"Dad!" he cried, surprised. "When did you get here?"

"At the beginning of the fourth inning," Mr. Mendez said.

José's face clouded. "Then you saw . . ." he started to say, but couldn't go on. How could he face his father when he'd gotten out three out of four times at bat?

MUDDERS   7
BULLS   8

"What do you want to say, son?" Mr. Mendez asked, putting his arm across José's shoulders.

"I wanted to make you proud of me," José blurted out. "I know I've been messing up lately, but I thought if I could hit .375, like you did when you played in the minors, I could make up for disappointing you. I—I'm sorry, Dad. I know I've let you down."

Mr. Mendez stopped short and looked down at José. "Is that why you've been so down in the mouth?" he exclaimed.

José sighed, then nodded.

"Listen, son," Mr. Mendez said, "I may be disappointed when you go against my wishes—like you did when you hit Mrs. Dooley's car—but I'm not disappointed in you. I trust you when you say you're sorry, and that's that. As far as Mrs. Dooley is concerned, I know you've worked hard to make it up to her. From what I hear," he added, smiling, "you even applied a little extra elbow grease to her car the other day."

271

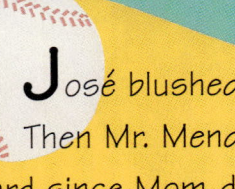

José blushed.

Then Mr. Mendez took a deep breath and went on: "It's been hard since Mom died . . . on all of us. I've had to depend on you and Carmen to pull your own weight . . . maybe too much." He grinned. "I seem to have forgotten how hard it can be to concentrate on anything when it's baseball season. Maybe we both need to be more aware of what the other person is feeling. I'll try, if you will."

José nodded happily.

"And one more thing. Forget about trying to hit like I did, okay? You don't have to. You're a born outfielder, José! You've made catches that I never would have been able to, not in a million years."

José stared at him. "Really? You mean you . . . don't mind that I can't hit?"

José's father chuckled. "'Can't hit?' If you call belting a grand slam homer not hitting, well, son, we've got to sit down and have a serious talk about the game of baseball! José, you're a born ballhawk, so stop worrying about the hitting and concentrate on your fielding. That's where your team needs you the most."

José couldn't believe his ears. All this time he had thought . . . but then he recalled the joyous cheers after each catch he had made that day and smiled.

"Thanks, Dad," he murmured. "I never thought about that. I just figured the guys were being nice when they said they counted on me being in the outfield." He glanced up at his father. "I like having people depend on me, Dad."

273

His father squeezed his shoulder. "Come on. We'll pick up some ice cream and celebrate those catches with Carmen. I understand she's had a hard afternoon, smashing one homer after another for her team. Looks like both of you kids are a chip off the old block, eh?"

José laughed. He never felt better in his life as he walked with his father to the car.

I might never get a .375 average, he thought. But I'm a hit with my father, and that's what counts the most.

Matt Christopher

Player:
Matt Christopher
Place of birth:
Bath, Pennsylvania
Hometown:
Rock Hill, South Carolina
First book:
The Lucky Baseball Bat
Favorite baseball position:
shortstop

Here's the author, Matt Christopher, as a young baseball player in 1937.

Matt Christopher can remember a time when he had troubles at bat just like José. When he was younger, he sometimes got discouraged because he wasn't a star hitter. Later he played on a semi-professional team and won an MVP (Most Valuable Player) award.

Now, instead of playing baseball, Matt Christopher writes about it. His characters include both boys and girls. "I see no reason why girls shouldn't play on boys' teams," the author says. "I've seen girls play better baseball than boys."

Yet, baseball isn't the only sport Mr. Christopher writes about. He has written more than seventy-five books. Some of them are about basketball, football, soccer, and track. "For a sport I haven't played, I do a lot of research," he says. To kids interested in writing, Mr. Christopher offers some advice. "Stick with it," says the author. "I wrote forty stories before I sold one."

Playing Outfield

by Isabel Joshlin Glaser

The baseball drops into your glove,
Sounds like . . . *Thunk!* (or *Plunk?*
Or *Plop? Whop?*) . . . but stays,
Sounds like . . . another sunny day,
Dust, sweat shivering down,
Clothes plastered to your skin,

THIRST . . . .

Sounds like you caught a flier,
The other side's out,
And your team leads,
Everybody's yelling like crazy,

HOORAY!

water, please . . .

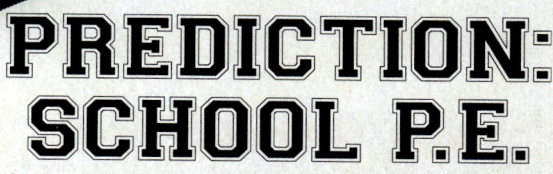

PREDICTION: SCHOOL P.E.

BY ISABEL JOSHLIN GLASER

Someday
when the baseball's
    hurtling
like some UFO,
    blazing
like some mad thing
    toward me
        in outfield
I *won't* gasp
and dodge. Oh, no!
Instead, I'll be
calmer than calm
    —so la-de-da!—
I'll just reach out
    like a *pro*
and catch it and—quick!—
    throw to second.
And everyone will say,
    "Hooray!
Natalie made a
    double-play!"
Some day.

RESPONSE

MAKE A POSTER

Sports Safety

Every sport has its own equipment and rules of play. Each sport also has rules of safety. Choose a sport that you have played or watched. Make a safety poster that tells players how to be safe. Display your poster in the classroom.

DESIGN A TRADING CARD

Personal Best

Major-league ballplayers have their pictures on trading cards. Design your own trading card. Paste a photograph of yourself on the front. If you can, use a photograph that shows you doing something you like to do. On the back side, tell things people would want to know about you. Trade cards with a classmate.

CORNER

WRITE A SPORTSCAST

Play-by-Play

Do you follow sports on radio or television? Sportscasters can make a game seem more exciting to viewers and listeners. Write an exciting sportscast of your own. Use what happened in the poem "Playing Outfield" or in a game you saw or played. Practice your sportscast. Then set up a "sports desk" in your classroom, and read your sportscast.

WHAT DO YOU THINK?

- Why does José think he needs to be a great batter?

- Do you think people need to be good at everything they do? Explain your answer.

- What did you like best about this story? Was there anything you didn't like?

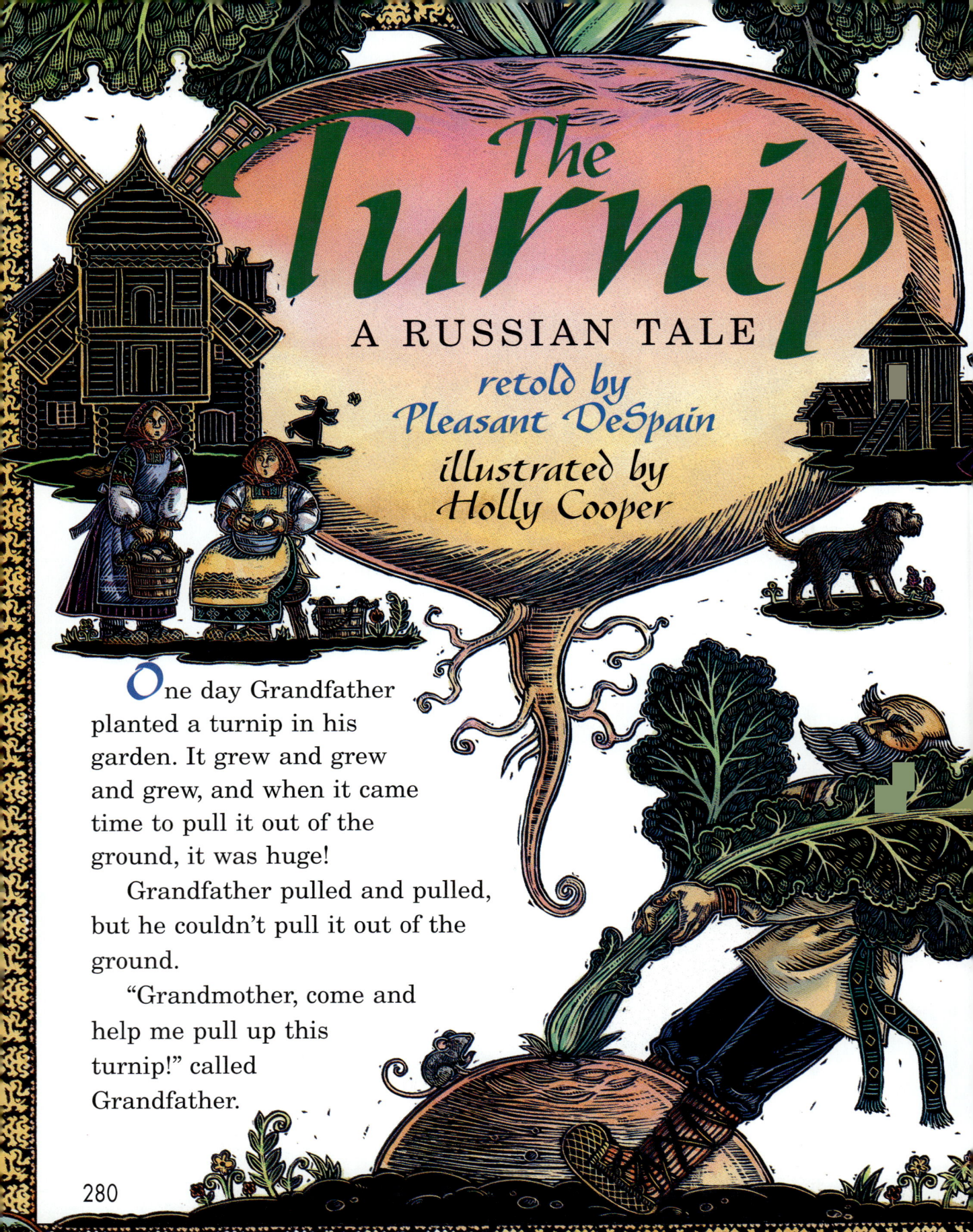

The Turnip

A RUSSIAN TALE

retold by
Pleasant DeSpain

illustrated by
Holly Cooper

One day Grandfather planted a turnip in his garden. It grew and grew and grew, and when it came time to pull it out of the ground, it was huge!

Grandfather pulled and pulled, but he couldn't pull it out of the ground.

"Grandmother, come and help me pull up this turnip!" called Grandfather.

Grandmother pulled on Grandfather and Grandfather pulled on the turnip. They pulled and pulled, but they couldn't pull it out of the ground.

Grandmother called to Mother, "Come and help us pull up this turnip!"

Mother pulled on Grandmother, Grandmother pulled on Grandfather, and Grandfather pulled on the turnip. They pulled and they pulled, but the turnip wouldn't budge.

"Daughter," called Mother, "come and help us pull up this turnip!"

Daughter pulled on Mother, Mother pulled on Grandmother, Grandmother pulled on Grandfather, and Grandfather pulled on the turnip. They pulled and they pulled, but it wouldn't move.

Daughter called to the dog, "Come and help us pull up this turnip!"

The dog pulled on Daughter, Daughter pulled on Mother, Mother pulled on Grandmother, Grandmother pulled on Grandfather, and Grandfather pulled on the turnip. They pulled and they pulled, but the turnip still wouldn't budge.

The dog barked to the cat, "Come and help us pull up this turnip!"

The cat pulled on the dog, the dog pulled on Daughter, Daughter pulled on Mother, Mother pulled on Grandmother, Grandmother pulled on Grandfather, and Grandfather pulled on the turnip. They pulled and they pulled, but they couldn't pull it out of the ground.

The cat meowed to the mouse, "Come and help us pull up this turnip!"

The mouse pulled on the cat, the cat pulled on the dog, the dog pulled on Daughter, Daughter pulled on Mother, Mother pulled on Grandmother, Grandmother pulled on Grandfather, and Grandfather pulled on the turnip. They pulled and they pulled, but they couldn't pull the turnip out of the ground.

The mouse squeaked to the beetle, "Come and help us pull up this turnip!"

The beetle pulled on the mouse, the mouse pulled on the cat, the cat pulled on the dog, the dog pulled on Daughter, Daughter pulled on Mother, Mother pulled on Grandmother, Grandmother pulled on Grandfather, and Grandfather pulled on the turnip. They pulled and they pulled, and they pulled the huge turnip right up out of the ground!

The turnip was so large that it fell on Grandfather and knocked him over! Grandfather fell on Grandmother! Grandmother fell on Mother! Mother fell on Daughter! Daughter fell on the dog! The dog fell on the cat! The cat fell on the mouse! The mouse fell on the beetle! And they all ate the turnip for supper.

After the Last Hard Freeze

by Arnold Adoff
illustrated by Jerry Pinkney

Award-Winning
Poet
and Illustrator

After The Last Hard Freeze   In Early Spring Weather

When The Ground Has Softened   And The Sun Is Strong
Enough To Warm The Open Field   We Dig Up The   Young
                                                                    Sumac
                                                                Saplings

From Their   Winter Places   Beside The Old
                                                            Fence

And Carry Them To   New
                                Places   In   Our   Front
                                                            Yard

I Am Digging Holes With Daddy Spreading Roots   Out
I Am Filling   Holes With Rich Dirt And Peat
                                                            Moss   Pouring
                                                                            In
                                            Green Fertilizer Water
                                            For A Healthy Start
                                            In Their New Homes

I Am Digging Holes With Daddy

ART AND LITERATURE

Detroit Industry is a mural that covers four walls. On this wall, people are working in an automobile factory. How does this artwork show the power of teamwork? If you painted a mural about teamwork, what would you show?

Detroit Industry (1933)
by Diego Rivera

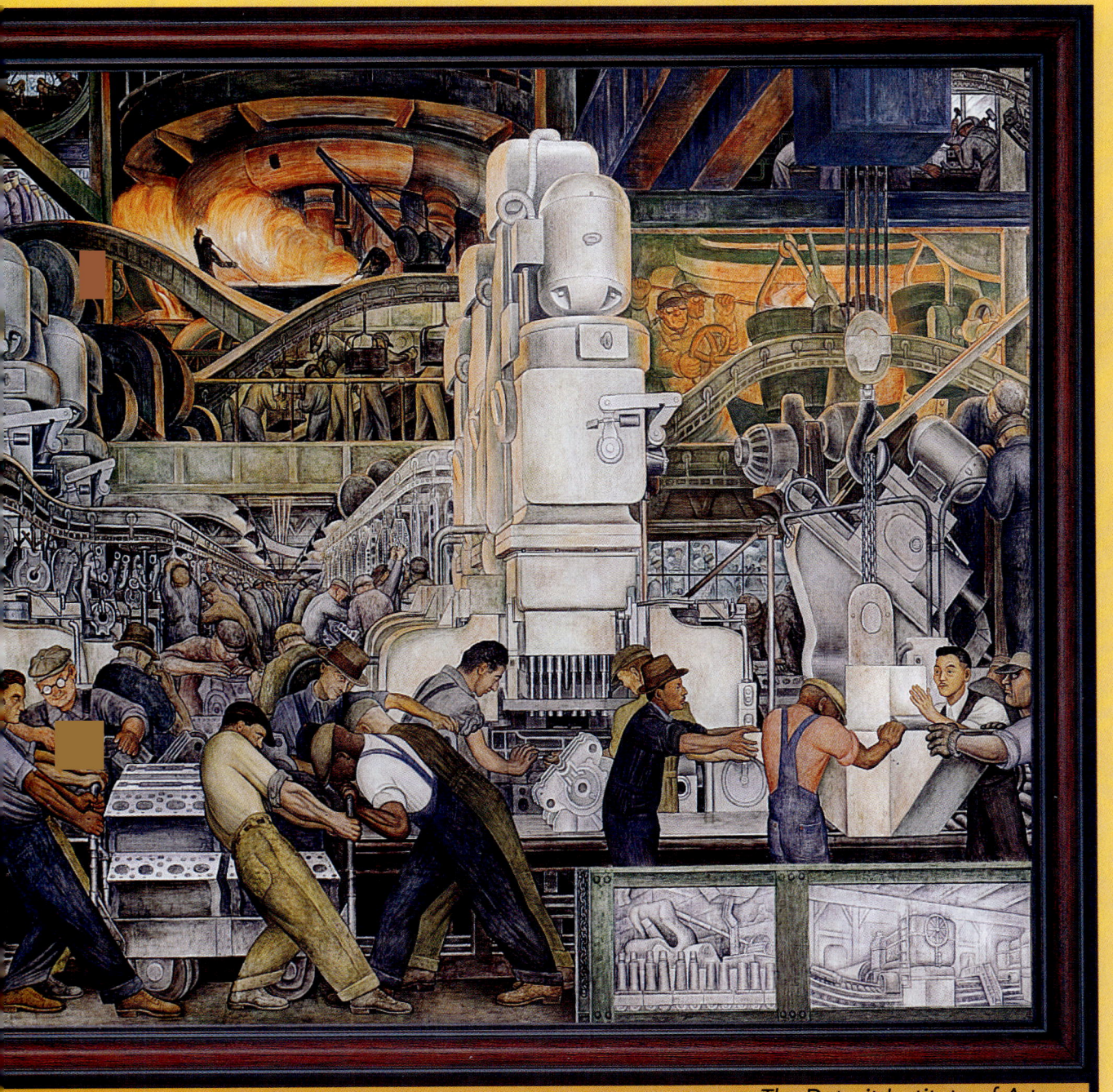

The Detroit Institute of Arts

Diego Rivera was a famous Mexican
artist who created many murals.
He often painted scenes that showed
the culture and history of Mexico.

Caldecott Medal
Children's Choice
SLJ Best Books

LON PO PO
A RED-RIDING HOOD STORY FROM CHINA
ED YOUNG

Lon Po Po

A Red-Riding Hood Story from China

translated and illustrated by

Ed Young

Once, long ago, there was a woman who lived alone in the country with her three children, Shang, Tao, and Paotze. On the day of their grandmother's birthday, the good mother set off to see her, leaving the three children at home.

Before she left, she said, "Be good while I am away, my heart-loving children; I will not return tonight. Remember to close the door tight at sunset and latch it well."

But an old wolf lived nearby and saw the good mother leave. At dusk, disguised as an old woman, he came up to the house of the children and knocked on the door twice: bang, bang.

Shang, who was the eldest, said through the latched door, "Who is it?"

"My little jewels," said the wolf, "this is your grandmother, your Po Po."

"Po Po!" Shang said. "Our mother has gone to visit you!"

The wolf acted surprised. "To visit me? I have not met her along the way. She must have taken a different route."

"Po Po!" Shang said. "How is it that you come so late?"

The wolf answered, "The journey is long, my children, and the day is short."

Shang listened through the door. "Po Po," she said, "why is your voice so low?"

"Your grandmother has caught a cold, good children, and it is dark and windy out here. Quickly open up, and let your Po Po come in," the cunning wolf said.

Tao and Paotze could not wait. One unlatched the door and the other opened it. They shouted, "Po Po, Po Po, come in!"

At the moment he entered the door, the wolf blew out the candle.

"Po Po," Shang asked, "why did you blow out the candle? The room is now dark."

The wolf did not answer.

Tao and Paotze rushed to their Po Po and wished to be hugged. The old wolf held Tao. "Good child, you are so plump." He embraced Paotze. "Good child, you have grown to be so sweet."

Soon the old wolf pretended to be sleepy. He yawned. "All the chicks are in the coop," he said. "Po Po is sleepy too." When he climbed into the big bed, Paotze climbed in at one end with the wolf, and Shang and Tao climbed in at the other.

But when Shang stretched, she touched the wolf's tail. "Po Po, Po Po, your foot has a bush on it."

"Po Po has brought hemp strings to weave you a basket," the wolf said.

Shang touched grandmother's sharp claws. "Po Po, Po Po, your hand has thorns on it."

"Po Po has brought an awl to make shoes for you," the wolf said.

At once, Shang lit the light and the wolf blew it out again, but Shang had seen the wolf's hairy face.

"Po Po, Po Po," she said, for she was not only the eldest, she was the most clever, "you must be hungry. Have you eaten gingko nuts?"

"What is gingko?" the wolf asked.

"Gingko is soft and tender, like the skin of a baby. One taste and you will live forever," Shang said, "and the nuts grow on the top of the tree just outside the door."

The wolf gave a sigh. "Oh, dear. Po Po is old, her bones have become brittle. No longer can she climb trees."

"Good Po Po, we can pick some for you," Shang said.

The wolf was delighted.

Shang jumped out of bed and Tao and Paotze came with her to the gingko tree. There, Shang told her sisters about the wolf and all three climbed up the tall tree.

The wolf waited and waited. Plump Tao did not come back. Sweet Paotze did not come back. Shang did not come back, and no one brought any nuts from the gingko tree. At last the wolf shouted, "Where are you, children?"

"Po Po," Shang called out, "we are on the top of the tree eating gingko nuts."

"Good children," the wolf begged, "pluck some for me."

"But Po Po, gingko is magic only when it is plucked directly from the tree. You must come and pluck it from the tree yourself."

The wolf came outside and paced back and forth under the tree where he heard the three children eating the gingko nuts at the top. "Oh, Po Po, these nuts are so tasty! The skin so tender," Shang said. The wolf's mouth began to water for a taste.

Finally, Shang, the eldest and most clever child, said, "Po Po, Po Po, I have a plan. At the door there is a big basket. Behind it is a rope. Tie the rope to the basket, sit in the basket and throw the other end to me. I can pull you up."

The wolf was overjoyed and fetched the basket and the rope, then threw one end of the rope to the top of the tree. Shang caught the rope and began to pull the basket up and up.

Halfway she let go of the rope, and the basket and the wolf fell to the ground.

"I am so small and weak, Po Po," Shang pretended. "I could not hold the rope alone."

"This time I will help," Tao said. "Let us do it again."

The wolf had only one thought in his mind: to taste a gingko nut. He climbed into the basket again. Now Shang and Tao pulled the rope on the basket together, higher and higher.

Again, they let go, and again the wolf tumbled down, down, and bumped his head.

The wolf was furious. He growled and cursed. "We could not hold the rope, Po Po," Shang said, "but only one gingko nut and you will be well again."

"I shall give a hand to my sisters this time," Paotze, the youngest, said. "This time we shall not fail."

Now the children pulled the rope with all of their strength. As they pulled they sang, "Hei yo, hei yo," and the basket rose straight up, higher than the first time, higher than the second time, higher and higher and higher until it nearly reached the top of the tree. When the wolf reached out, he could almost touch the highest branch.

But at that moment, Shang coughed and they all let go of the rope, and the basket fell down and down and down. Not only did the wolf bump his head, but he broke his heart to pieces.

"Po Po," Shang shouted, but there was no answer.

"Po Po," Tao shouted, but there was no answer.

"Po Po," Paotze shouted. There was still no answer. The children climbed to the branches just above the wolf and saw that he was truly dead. Then they climbed down, went into the house, closed the door, locked the door with the latch and fell peacefully asleep.

On the next day, their mother returned with baskets of food from their real Po Po, and the three sisters told her the story of the Po Po who had come.

About the Author and Illustrator

Ed Young

Ed Young was born in China in 1931, the Chinese Year of the Sheep. As a boy, he had a busy imagination. "I drew everything that happened to cross my mind," he remembers, "airplanes, people, a tall ship that my father was very proud of, a hunter, and a bird dog that came out of my head—I have always been happiest doing my own thing. Sometimes I played alone for hours without a toy or prop in an empty room."

When Ed Young was twenty years old, he came to the United States. He studied art and worked for magazines. A few years later, he began to illustrate children's books.

Making the illustrations for *Lon Po Po* took some special thinking. To make his drawings look real, Mr. Young had to learn about wolves. He also had to remember how the children in China lived and even how the trees grew.

Ed Young thinks the story and pictures need to work together to make a good book. "There are things that words can do that pictures never can," he says. He also thinks there are pictures that words can never describe. The story and pictures together should do what neither one can do alone.

Response Corner

CREATE A MESSAGE

Spread the Word

How many times have you heard people say, "Don't open the door when you are alone"? The girls in "Lon Po Po" broke this rule. Brainstorm safety tips that everyone should know. Then choose a few tips, and create a billboard message. Use interesting words and pictures to help people remember your message.

Po Po or Grandma?

In China, children often call their grandmother *Po Po*. Children from different cultures have other special names for their grandparents. Ask the members of your class what they call their grandparents. Make a bar graph showing how many people use each name. Talk about what the graph shows.

Happily Ever After

"Lon Po Po" is very much like the story "Little Red Riding-Hood." Which story do you like better? Write a paragraph that tells how the two stories are alike and how they are different. Then write a paragraph that tells which one you like better and explains why.

WHAT DO YOU THINK?

- What mistake do Tao and Paotze make? What happens because of this mistake?

- What would you have done when the wolf knocked on the door?

- How do you think the girls' mother felt when she returned? Explain your answer.

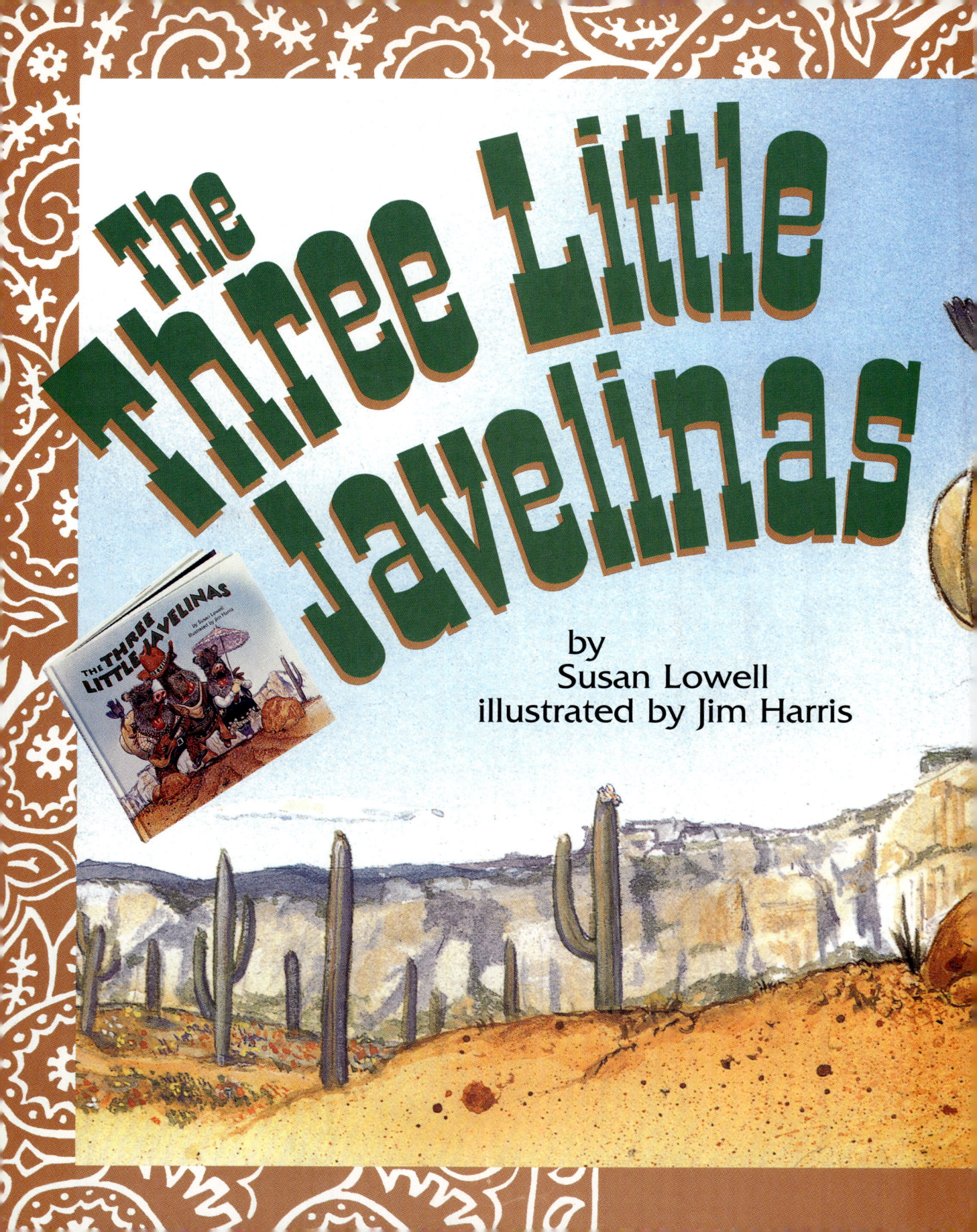

The Three Little Javelinas

by
Susan Lowell
illustrated by Jim Harris

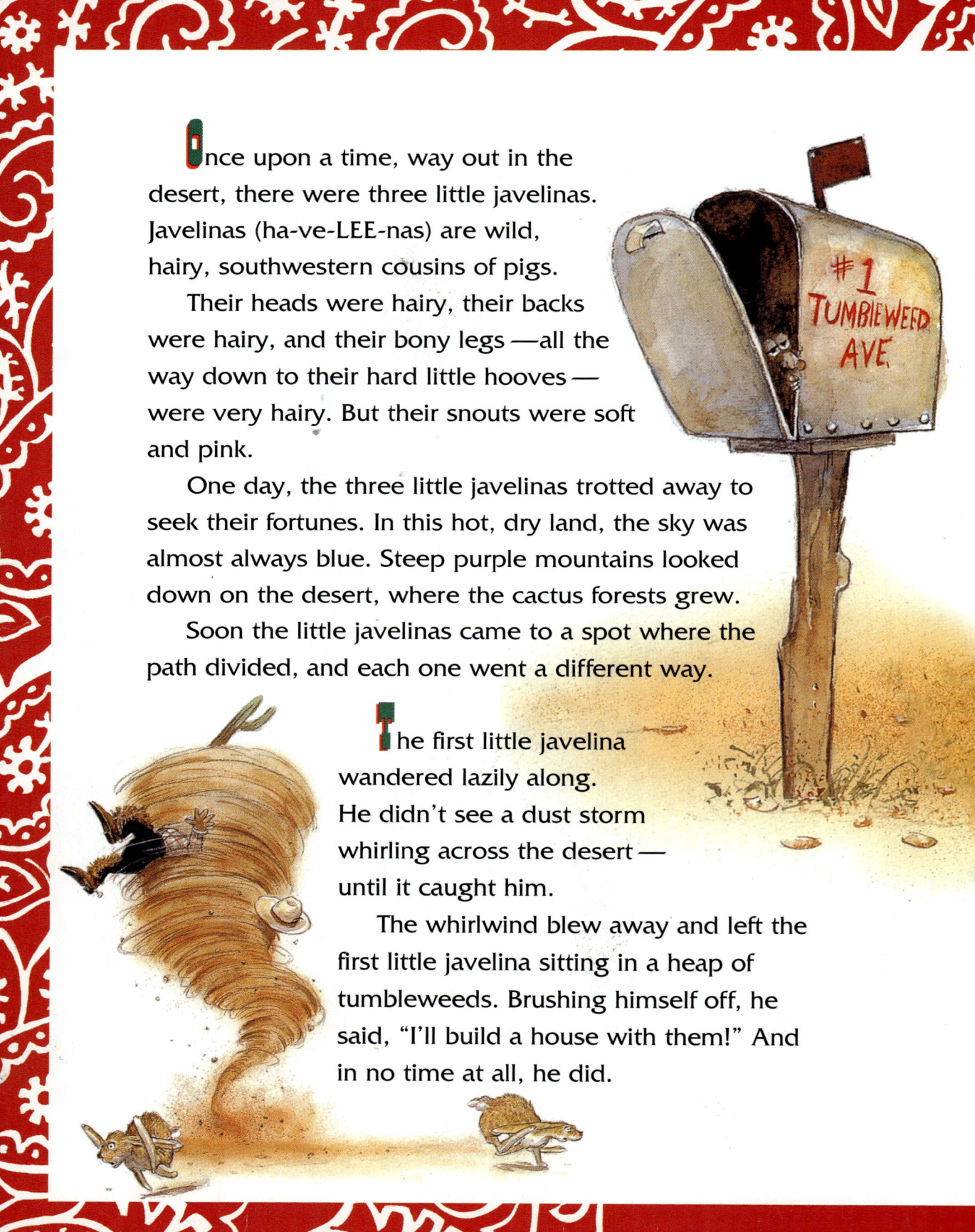

Once upon a time, way out in the desert, there were three little javelinas. Javelinas (ha-ve-LEE-nas) are wild, hairy, southwestern cousins of pigs.

Their heads were hairy, their backs were hairy, and their bony legs —all the way down to their hard little hooves — were very hairy. But their snouts were soft and pink.

One day, the three little javelinas trotted away to seek their fortunes. In this hot, dry land, the sky was almost always blue. Steep purple mountains looked down on the desert, where the cactus forests grew.

Soon the little javelinas came to a spot where the path divided, and each one went a different way.

The first little javelina wandered lazily along. He didn't see a dust storm whirling across the desert — until it caught him.

The whirlwind blew away and left the first little javelina sitting in a heap of tumbleweeds. Brushing himself off, he said, "I'll build a house with them!" And in no time at all, he did.

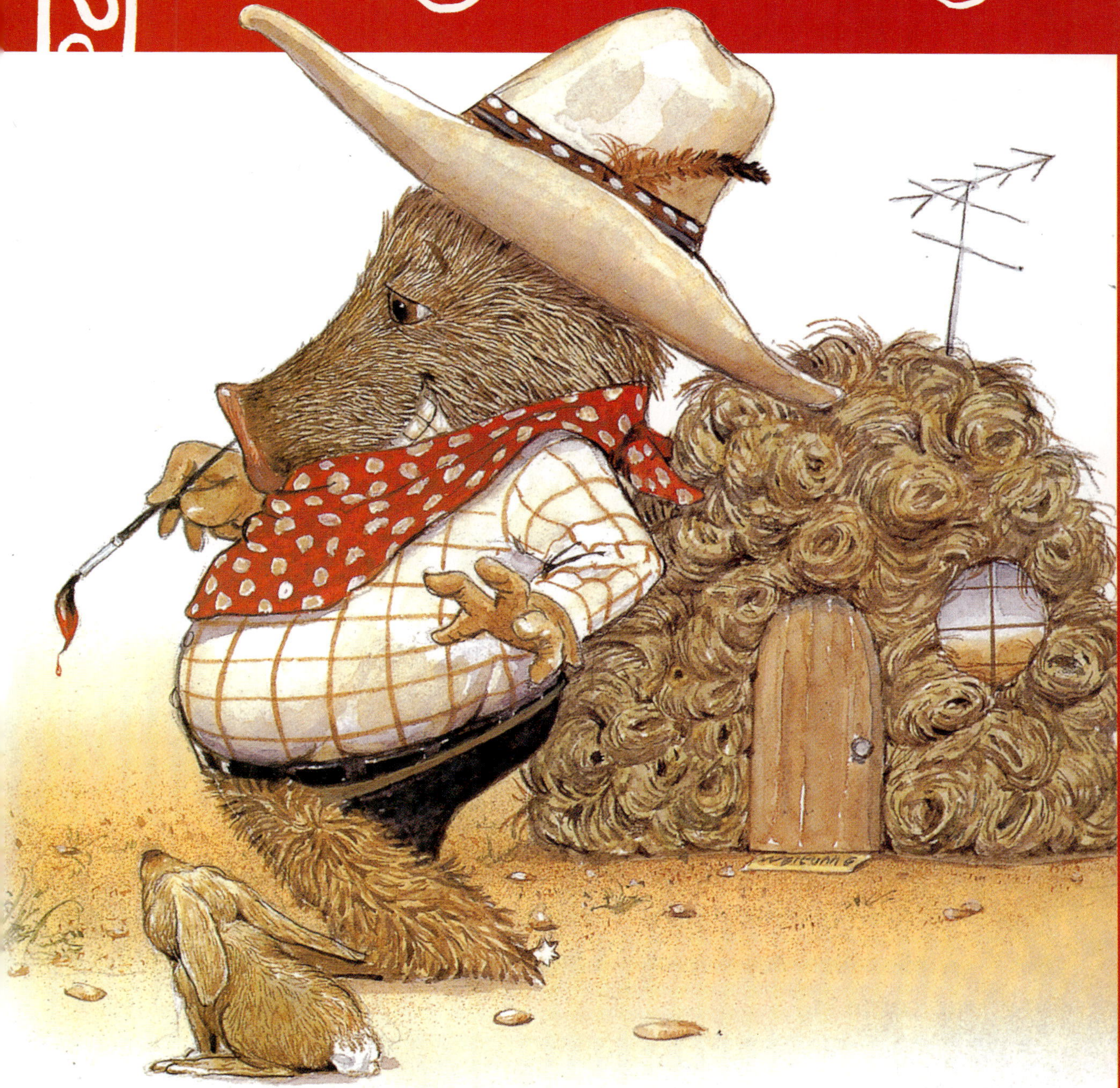

Then along came a coyote. He ran through the desert so quickly and so quietly that he was almost invisible. In fact, this was only one of Coyote's many magical tricks. He laughed when he saw the tumbleweed house and smelled the javelina inside.

"Mmm! A tender juicy piggy!" he thought. Coyote was tired of eating mice and rabbits.

He called out sweetly, "Little pig, little pig, let me come in."

"Not by the hair of my chinny-chin-chin!" shouted the first javelina (who had a lot of hair on his chinny-chin-chin!).

"Then I'll huff, and I'll puff, and I'll blow your house in!" said Coyote.

And he huffed, and he puffed, and he blew the little tumbleweed house away.

But in all the hullabaloo, the first little javelina
escaped—and went looking for his brother and sister.
Coyote, who was very sneaky, tiptoed along behind.

The second little javelina walked for miles among giant cactus plants called saguaros (sa-WA-ros). They held their ripe red fruit high in the sky. But they made almost no shade, and the little javelina grew hot.

Then he came upon a Native American woman who was gathering sticks from inside a dried-up cactus. She planned to use these long sticks, called saguaro ribs, to knock down the sweet cactus fruit.

The second little javelina said, "Please, may I have some sticks to build a house?"

"*Ha'u,*" (ha-ou) she said, which means "yes" in the language of the Desert People.

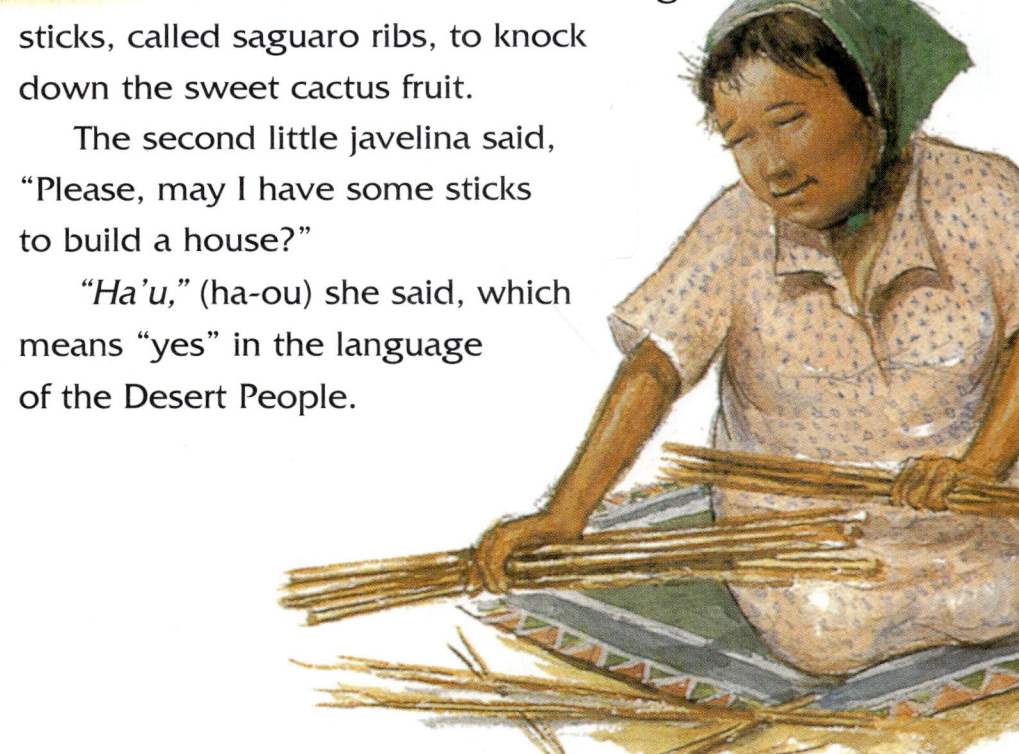

When he was finished building his house, he lay down in the shade. Then his brother arrived, panting from the heat, and the second little javelina moved over and made a place for him.

Pretty soon, Coyote found the saguaro rib house. He used his magic to make his voice sound just like another javelina's.

"Little pig, little pig, let me come in!" he called.

But the little javelinas were suspicious. The second one cried, "No! Not by the hair of my chinny-chin-chin!"

"Bah!" thought Coyote. "I am not going to eat your hair."

Then Coyote smiled, showing all his sharp teeth: "I'll huff, and I'll puff, and I'll blow your house in!"

So he huffed, and he puffed, and all the saguaro ribs came tumbling down.

But the two little javelinas escaped into the desert.
Still not discouraged, Coyote followed. Sometimes his
magic did fail, but then he usually came up with another trick.

The third little
javelina trotted through
beautiful palo verde trees,
with green trunks and yellow
flowers. She saw a snake sliding
by, smooth as oil. A hawk floated
round and round above her. Then
she came to a place where a man was making adobe
(a-DOE-be) bricks from mud and straw. The bricks lay
on the ground, baking in the hot sun.

The third little javelina thought for a moment, and said, "May I please have a few adobes to build a house?"

"*Sí,*" answered the man, which means "yes" in Spanish, the brick-maker's language.

So the third javelina built herself a solid little adobe house, cool in summer and warm in winter. When her brothers found her, she welcomed them in and locked the door behind them.

Coyote followed their trail.

"Little pig, little pig, let me come in!" he called.

The three little javelinas looked out the window. This time Coyote pretended to be very old and weak, with no teeth and a sore paw. But they were not fooled.

"No! Not by the hair of my chinny-chin-chin," called back the third little javelina.

"Then I'll huff, and I'll puff, and I'll blow your house in!" said Coyote. He grinned, thinking of the wild pig dinner to come.

"Just try it!" shouted the third little javelina.

So Coyote huffed and puffed, but the adobe bricks did not budge.

Again, Coyote tried. "I'LL HUFF. . . AND I'LL
PUFF. . . AND I'LL BLOW YOUR HOUSE IN!"

The three little javelinas covered their hairy ears.
But nothing happened. The javelinas peeked out
the window.

The tip of Coyote's raggedy tail whisked right past their noses. He was climbing upon the tin roof. Next, Coyote used his magic to make himself very skinny.

"The stove pipe!" gasped the third little javelina. Quickly she lighted a fire inside her wood stove.

"What a feast it will be!" Coyote said to himself. He squeezed into the stove pipe. "I think I'll eat them with red hot chile sauce!"

Whoosh. S-s-sizzle!

Then the three little javelinas heard an amazing noise. It was not a bark. It was not a cackle. It was not a howl. It was not a scream. It was all of those sounds together. YIP YAP YEEP

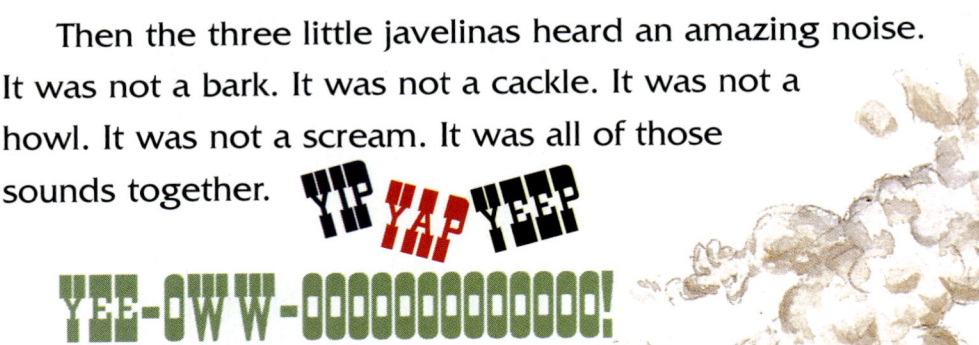

YEE-OWW-OOOOOOOOOOOOO!

Away ran a puff of smoke shaped like a coyote.

The three little javelinas lived happily ever after in the adobe house.

And if you ever hear Coyote's voice, way out in the desert at night . . . well, you know what he's remembering!

POSTCARDS FROM THE AUTHOR

Dear Readers,

Greetings from my home in the Sonoran Desert in Arizona! There are desert areas like this in parts of California, Texas, and New Mexico, too—as well as in northern Mexico. I can see javelinas, coyotes, tumbleweeds, and cacti from my windows!

The history of this part of the United States is rooted in Native American and Spanish cultures. The little javelinas' houses are like houses that have been built here for hundreds of years.

Why don't you write a story about where *you* live? Have fun!

Your friend,

Susan Lowell

Susan Lowell

FROM THE ILLUSTRATOR

Hi, Kids!

This is my home in Colorado, where I live on the north face of the Grand Mesa, the biggest flat-topped mountain in the world. This mountain is almost 11,000 feet high. From my windows I can look down into beautiful valleys.

My house is at the end of a dirt road. The stars seem to shine very brightly here, because there aren't any other lights nearby.

Elk and deer wander onto my deck, and at night my family and I can sometimes hear coyotes howl. But guess what! No javelinas. They're in the Southwest.

Happy reading,

Jim Harris

Response Corner

A SIGHTSEEING TRIP

Create a journal for a week-long trip through the Southwest. In your journal, write about what you see and hear along the way. Give the names of cities you go through and the number of miles you travel. You can use a map and the story to help you. Watch out for javelinas!

MAKE A CLASS BOOK

DIFFERENT HOUSES

You know that there are adobe houses in the Southwest. With your classmates, put together a class book about other kinds of houses. Describe houses that are common to where you live or common to other areas. Use home and travel magazines and an encyclopedia to help you. Draw or cut out pictures to add to your class book. Tell why each kind of house is right for its place.

BRING A HAMMER AND NAILS

One of the javelinas was smart enough to build a strong house. Imagine that you want to build one, too. Write a want ad for a builder. In the ad, tell what skills the builder should have and what work experience would be helpful. In your ad, explain why the job is important.

WHAT DO YOU THINK?

- According to this story, why do coyotes howl?

- Which little javelina do you like the most? Why?

- Have you ever read or heard another story like this? How was it the same? How was it different?

The characters and the real people in this theme work together—in silly ways and in serious ways. What did you learn from these selections about working together?

"Lon Po Po" and "The Three Little Javelinas" are both about good characters working against a bad character. How else are the two stories alike?

WRAP-UP

ACTIVITY CORNER

When you play on a sports team, each team member has a special part to play. Form a group to do some other kind of work, such as a school assignment or a clean-up project. Before you start, decide which group member will do each part of the job.

Glossary

WHAT IS A GLOSSARY?

A glossary is like a small dictionary at the back of a book. It lists some of the words used in the book, along with their pronunciations, their meanings, and other useful information. If you come across a word you don't know as you are reading, you can look up the word in this glossary.

Using the

Like a dictionary, this glossary lists words in alphabetical order. To find a word, look it up by its first letter or letters.

To save time, use the **guide words** at the top of each page. These show you the first and last words on the page. Look at the guide words to see if your word falls between them alphabetically.

Here is an example of a glossary entry:

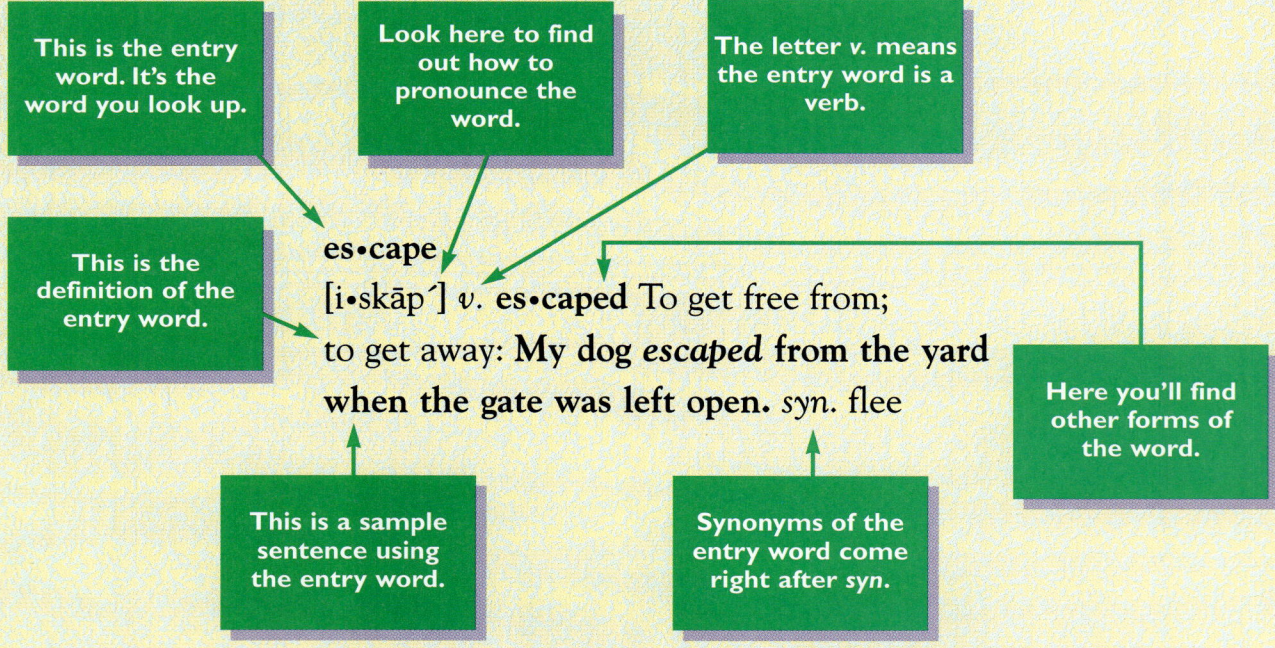

This is the entry word. It's the word you look up.

Look here to find out how to pronounce the word.

The letter *v.* means the entry word is a verb.

This is the definition of the entry word.

es•cape
[i•skāp´] *v.* **es•caped** To get free from; to get away: **My dog** *escaped* **from the yard when the gate was left open.** *syn.* flee

This is a sample sentence using the entry word.

Synonyms of the entry word come right after *syn.*

Here you'll find other forms of the word.

ETYMOLOGY

Etymology is the study or history of how words are developed. Words often have interesting backgrounds that can help you remember what they mean. Look in the margins of the glossary to find the etymologies of certain words.

Here is an example of an etymology:

crane   *Crane* is also the name of a long-necked bird. The big machine used for lifting heavy things got its name because it looks like the bird.

Glossary

PRONUNCIATION

The pronunciation in brackets is a respelling that shows how the word is pronounced.

The **pronunciation key** explains what the symbols in a respelling mean. A shortened pronunciation key appears on every other page of the glossary.

PRONUNCIATION KEY*

a	add, map	m	move, seem	u	up, done
ā	ace, rate	n	nice, tin	û(r)	burn, term
â(r)	care, air	ng	ring, song	yo͞o	fuse, few
ä	palm, father	o	odd, hot	v	vain, eve
b	bat, rub	ō	open, so	w	win, away
ch	check, catch	ô	order, jaw	y	yet, yearn
d	dog, rod	oi	oil, boy	z	zest, muse
e	end, pet	ou	pout, now	zh	vision, pleasure
ē	equal, tree	o͝o	took, full	ə	the schwa, an
f	fit, half	o͞o	pool, food		unstressed vowel
g	go, log	p	pit, stop		representing the
h	hope, hate	r	run, poor		sound spelled
i	it, give	s	see, pass		*a* in *above*
ī	ice, write	sh	sure, rush		e in *sicken*
j	joy, ledge	t	talk, sit		*i* in *possible*
k	cool, take	th	thin, both		o in *melon*
l	look, rule	t̶h̶	this, bathe		*u* in *circus*

Other symbols:
- • separates words into syllables
- ´ indicates heavier stress on a syllable
- ˎ indicates light stress on a syllable

Abbreviations: *adj.* adjective, *adv.* adverb, *conj.* conjunction, *interj.* interjection, *n.* noun, *prep.* preposition, *pron.* pronoun, *syn.* synonym, *v.* verb.

*The Pronunciation Key, adapted entries, and the Short Key that appear on the following pages are reprinted from *HBJ School Dictionary* Copyright © 1990 by Harcourt Brace & Company. Reprinted by permission of Harcourt Brace & Company.

active The words *active, act, action,* and *actor* all come from a Latin word meaning "to do or perform." However, *player* was used in the theater until the sixteenth century, when it changed to *actor.*

advise *Advise* comes from a Latin word meaning "in my view." The French gave it the meaning "in my opinion." In English, it means "to give information."

a•chiev•er
[ə•chēv´er] *n.* Someone who does what he or she tries to do; someone who reaches a goal: **Teresa is a high achiever because she does her best and gets good grades.**

ac•tive
[ak´tiv] *adj.* Working; busy; full of life and doing things: **Owls sleep during the day and are active at night.**

ad•vise
[ad•vīz´] *v.* To tell someone what to do or how to do it: **The coach is going to advise his players about how to hit a baseball.**
syns. recommend; inform

an•kle
[ang´kəl] *n.* **an•kles** The bony area between a person's leg and foot: **It had rained all afternoon, and the puddles were up to Misha's ankles.**

a•ware
[ə•wâr´] *adj.* In a state of knowing; understanding fully: **Tracy was not aware that the car was coming toward her, until her friend shouted to her.**
syn. alert

cap•ture
[kap´chər] *v.* To catch: **Josh knew not to capture the beautiful butterfly because there are too few of them left already.** *syns.* take; trap

ca•reer

[kə•rir´] *n.* A person's life work; a job one trains for or studies for and then does for a long time: **Ahmad had an interesting** *career* **as an author of children's books.**

cel•e•brate

[sel´ə•brāt´] *v.* **cel•e•brat•ed** To take part in a holiday activity or a party: **We** *celebrated* **the Fourth of July with music and ice cream.**
syns. observe; rejoice

con•cen•trate

[kon´sən•trāt´] *v.* To pay attention to only one thing; to think about something very hard: **When I study my science lesson, I need to** *concentrate.*
syn. focus

coun•try•side

[kun´trē•sīd´] *n.* Land outside the city: **The** *countryside* **is pretty because lots of trees and grass cover the land.**

cous•in

[kuz´(ə)n] *n.* **cous•ins** Something or someone that is like or in the same family as another: **Even though large pandas look like bears, pandas are actually** *cousins* **of the raccoon.**

crane

[krān] *n.* A big tractor-like machine with a long arm used to lift and move things: **They used a** *crane* **to lift the heavy pole and put it in a truck that would take it away.**

cun•ning

[kun´ing] *adj.* Clever and tricky; smart in a sneaky way: **My cat is very** *cunning* **and will drink your milk when you are not looking.**

countryside

crane *Crane* is also the name of a long-necked bird. The big machine used for lifting heavy things got its name because it looks like the bird.

a	add	o͝o	took
ā	ace	o͞o	pool
â	care	u	up
ä	palm	û	burn
e	end	yo͞o	fuse
ē	equal	oi	oil
i	it	ou	pout
ī	ice	ng	ring
o	odd	th	thin
ō	open	t̶h̶	this
ô	order	zh	vision

ə = {
a in *above*
e in *sicken*
i in *possible*
o in *melon*
u in *circus*
}

damage The English word is the same as the original French word *damage*. But the French changed it to *dommage*.

daydream

D

dam·age
[dam´ij] *n.* The hurt caused by an action; a loss of or harm to something: **The fire caused a lot of *damage* to the barn.** *syn.* injury

day·dream
[dā´drēm´] *v.* **day·dreamed** To imagine nice thoughts or wishes; to think about pleasant ideas in a wishful way: **Latisha *daydreamed* about the great things she will do when she grows up.**

de·pend
[di·pend´] *v.* To trust; to need someone or something: **I *depend* on you to help your little sister with her homework.** *syn.* rely

des·ert
[dez´ərt] *n.* A very dry place that may be covered with sand and has few plants: **The *desert* is very hot in the daytime, but it cools down at night.**

dif·fer·ent·ly
[dif´ə·rənt·lē] *adv.* Not in the same way: **Juan combs his hair *differently* than his twin does, and it helps people tell them apart.** *syn.* distinctly

dis·ap·pear
[dis´ə·pir´] *v.* **dis·ap·peared** To go out of sight: **Betty watched as the plane *disappeared* into the sky.** *syn.* vanish

dis·ap·point·ed
[dis´ə·point´id] *adj.* Not getting what you wanted or hoped for; let down; feeling unhappy: **Susan was *disappointed* that the rain kept her from going outside.** *syn.* dissatisfied

drab

[drab] *adj.* Boring looking; uninteresting or dull in color: **Other people said the weather was** *drab,* **but Dennis loved the gray, rainy days.**

drift

[drift] *v.* **drift•ed** To move back and forth slowly through the air: **The leaves** *drifted* **down from the trees.**

dusk

[dusk] *n.* The time just before night falls; after sunset and before dark: **All the streetlights go on at** *dusk,* **before it gets too dark.**

E

e•lec•tric•i•ty

[i•lek´tris´ə•tē] *n.* Something that gives power to make things work; the flow of charges through a substance, such as a wire, used to run things: ***Electricity* is used to keep our stove and refrigerator going.**

es•cape

[i•skāp´] *v.* **es•caped** To get free from; to get away: **My dog** *escaped* **from the yard when the gate was left open.** *syn.* flee

F

fault

[fôlt] *n.* The cause of a problem: **The bus was late, so it was not our** *fault* **we missed the school bell.** *syn.* blame

escape *Escape* **comes from a Latin word meaning "to take off one's coat." The English decided it means "to get one's freedom."**

a	add	o͝o	took
ā	ace	o͞o	pool
â	care	u	up
ä	palm	û	burn
e	end	yo͞o	fuse
ē	equal	oi	oil
i	it	ou	pout
ī	ice	ng	ring
o	odd	th	thin
ō	open	t̶h̶	this
ô	order	zh	vision

ə = {
a in *above*
e in *sicken*
i in *possible*
o in *melon*
u in *circus*
}

fortune

fortune The Roman god of luck was called *Fortuna*. If she was on your side, you were considered *fortunate*.

harbor

jewel

for·tune

[fôr´chən] *n.* **for·tunes**
Luck or chance; success; wealth: **After finishing high school, they left the farm to find their** *fortunes* **in the big city.**

fright·en

[frīt´ən] *v.* **fright·ened**
To make afraid; to be made afraid: **The baby was** *frightened* **by the loud noises.** *syn.* scare

fro·zen

[frō´zən] *adj.* Not moving; being still: **When he saw the bear, he stood** *frozen* **in his tracks.**

har·bor

[här´bər] *n.* A part of the ocean, near land, where ships stay and are safe: **As the storm rolled in, more ships sailed into the** *harbor* **to be safe.** *syn.* port

im·i·tate

[im´ə·tāt´] *v.* To copy something to make it look the same; to use as an example: **Brad liked the way his brother danced and tried to** *imitate* **him at the party.** *syn.* mimic

im·pos·si·ble

[im·pos´ə·bəl] *adj.*
Unable to be done; not able to happen: **It's** *impossible* **to be in two places at one time.** *syn.* unworkable

jew·el

[jōō´əl] *n.* A stone that is usually worth money; something that is worth a lot: **The ring with the bright red** *jewel* **in it cost a lot of money.**

L

light•ning
[līt´ning] *n.* A sudden bright flash in the sky caused by an electrical charge from storm clouds: **The weather report said there would be a lot of** *lightning* **during the storm.**

P

pack•age
[pak´ij] *n.* Something that is wrapped up or boxed: **Mario was able to fit the card into the large** *package* **of fruit that was being sent to his grandparents.**

pas•ture
[pas´chər] *n.* Ground covered with grass for animals to eat: **From the road, Minh could see cows eating in a** *pasture.*

pe•ti•tion
[pə•tish´ən] *n.* A paper people can sign that asks for something from someone in charge: **The students have a** *petition* **asking the school for more computers.**

pho•to•graph
[fō´tə•graf´] *n.* **pho•to•graphs** A picture made with a camera: **We took lots of** *photographs* **of the Grand Canyon on our vacation to Arizona.**

lightning

photograph
Photograph comes from *photo,* meaning "light," and *graph,* meaning "write." Photography is something like "writing with light."

a	add	o͝o	took
ā	ace	o͞o	pool
â	care	u	up
ä	palm	û	burn
e	end	yo͞o	fuse
ē	equal	oi	oil
i	it	ou	pout
ī	ice	ng	ring
o	odd	th	thin
ō	open	t̶h̶	this
ô	order	zh	vision

ə = {
a in *above*
e in *sicken*
i in *possible*
o in *melon*
u in *circus*

pluck

pluck

property

realize *Realize* comes from the word *real*. In English *real* was first used to mean "property," and that is where we get the term *real estate*. Later, *real* took on the meaning of "something that actually exists."

pluck
[pluk] *v.* To pull off; to pull out: **I *pluck* the flowers from the garden and put them in a vase.** *syn.* pick

plump
[plump] *adj.* A little fat; having a rounded shape: **The little piglets were *plump,* just like their mother.** *syn.* chubby

pro·gram
[prō´gram´] *n.* A planned way to do something; steps to follow to do something; an organized activity: **Phyllis is going to join the after-school basketball *program.*** *syns.* procedure, organization

prop·er·ty
[prop´ər·tē] *n.* A piece of land; something owned by a person or a group: **The *property* our house is on is small, so we do not have a big yard.** *syn.* holdings

re·al·ize
[rē´əl·īz´] *v.* **re·al·ized** To understand; to come to know: **They *realized* the big dog was really very friendly, even though it barked loudly.**

re·call
[ri·kôl´] *v.* To remember; to think about again; to bring to mind again: **Debbie tried to *recall* where she had left her book.** *syn.* recollect

re•cord

[rek´ərd] *n.* **re•cords**
Information about a
person or business:
**School *records* tell
about the students,
their grades, and their
behavior.** *syn.* document

rel•a•tive

[rel´ə•tiv] *n.* **rel•a•tives**
A person in the same
family: **My aunts, my
uncles, and all of my
other *relatives* brought
me presents when they
came to my birthday
party.** *syn.* kin

re•spon•si•ble

[ri•spon´sə•bəl] *adj.*
Being the cause of
something; being the
person in charge of
something: **Tomika is
responsible for having
made the signs too small,
and she will fix them.**

sci•en•tist

[sī´ən•tist] *n.* **sci•en•tists**
A person who studies
nature and life: **Some
scientists study the
Earth, the stars, the
moon, and the sun.**

shad•ow

[shad´ō] *n.* **shad•ows**
A dark area, where light
is cut off: **The tree
blocks the sun, so we
keep cool by sitting in
the *shadows* underneath
the tree.** *syn.* shade

shiv•er

[shiv´ər] *v.* **shiv•ered** To
shake from fear or cold:
**In the spooky old
house, Curtis *shivered*
when he heard strange
noises outside his door.**

soar

[sôr] *v.* **soar•ing** To fly
high: **The kite was
soaring high in the air.**

scientist

shadow *Shadow*
comes from *shade*,
which is related to
the word *shed*. *Shed*
used to mean "a
roof held up by
poles." In hot
weather, one would
go under a *shed* to
get in the *shade*.

a	add	ŏŏ	took
ā	ace	ōō	pool
â	care	u	up
ä	palm	û	burn
e	end	yōō	fuse
ē	equal	oi	oil
i	it	ou	pout
ī	ice	ng	ring
o	odd	th	thin
ō	open	t͟h	this
ô	order	zh	vision

ə = {
a in *above*
e in *sicken*
i in *possible*
o in *melon*
u in *circus*

squeeze

sunset

spar•kle
[spar´kəl] *v.* **spar•kling**
To shine; to glitter:
Everyone in the room could see her crown *sparkling* **as she danced with the prince.** *syns.* glisten, twinkle

sprin•kle
[spring´kəl] *v.* **sprin•kling**
To drop or throw tiny pieces around gently: **Ted likes** *sprinkling* **cheese on his chili.** *syn.* scatter

squeeze
[skwēz] *v.* To press; to push together: **I like to** *squeeze* **oranges in order to make fresh orange juice.** *syn.* crush

stub•born
[stub´ərn] *adj.* Not willing to change one's mind; not giving in: **Diane was so** *stubborn* **that she would not even try the new game.** *syn.* unbending

suc•cess
[sək•ses´] *n.* The state of getting good results; a person who is good at something or is well known: **When Darnell won the spelling bee, he knew he was a** *success.*

sun•set
[sun´set´] *n.* The time when the sun goes down, just before it turns dark: **At** *sunset,* **we pick up our toys and go inside.**

tear
[târ] *v.* **tears** To move very fast: **Greg** *tears* **down the street on his bicycle in a hurry to meet his friends.** *syns.* race, rush

thun·der

[thun´dər] *n.* The loud booming sound that comes from the sky during a storm: **Our dog hid under the bed because the *thunder* scared him.**

tum·ble·weed

[tum´bəl·wēd´] *n.* **tum·ble·weeds** A round bush that grows in flat, dry areas without trees and that, when dead, is blown around by the wind: **The *tumbleweeds* had dried up and were light, so the wind blew them across the ranch and into the fence.**

van·ish

[van´ish] *v.* To go out of sight: **As soon as my dog heard the bathwater running, he would *vanish*.** *syn.* disappear

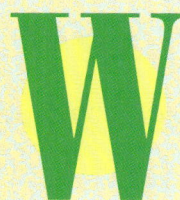

weave

[wēv] *v.* To make something by crossing long pieces of material, such as cloth or rope, over and under each other: **Rosa's grandmother showed her how to *weave* a rug out of strips of cloth.**

weave

thunder *Thunder* comes from a word meaning "noise." Thor was the Nordic god of thunder who drove his chariot across the sky with a great rumbling noise. A day was named after him. *Thursday* is "Thor's day."

tumbleweed

a	add	o͝o	took
ā	ace	o͞o	pool
â	care	u	up
ä	palm	û	burn
e	end	yo͞o	fuse
ē	equal	oi	oil
i	it	ou	pout
ī	ice	ng	ring
o	odd	th	thin
ō	open	th	this
ô	order	zh	vision

ə = {
a in *above*
e in *sicken*
i in *possible*
o in *melon*
u in *circus*

INDEX OF
Titles and Authors

Page numbers in color refer to biographical information.

Ada, Alma Flor, **216,** 230

Adoff, Arnold, **284**

After the Last Hard Freeze, **284**

Appelemando's Dreams, **60**

Ardley, Neil, **88**

Brave Irene, **114**

Centerfield Ballhawk, **264**

Christopher, Matt, **264,** 275

City Green, **242**

Cooper, Ilene, **96,** 103

DeFord, Deborah H., **258**

DeSpain, Pleasant, **280**

DiSalvo-Ryan, DyAnne, **242,** 255

Dorros, Arthur, **18,** 38

Faust, Naomi F., **104**

Glaser, Isabel Joshlin, **276, 277**

Hesse, Karen, **178,** 206

How a Girl Got Her Chinese Name, **232**

Isla, **18**

Jerry Pinkney: Achiever of Dreams, **96**

Kids and Kicks, **258**

Lester's Dog, **178**

Lon Po Po, **288**

London, Jonathan, **174**

Lowell, Susan, **312,** 328

Makley, Mike, **262**

Milios, Rita, **42**

My Name Is María Isabel, **216**

Mystery of the Sounds in the Night, The, **162**

New Kid, The, **262**

Nixon, Joan Lowery, **162**

Parent to Child, **104**

Playing Outfield, **276**

Polacco, Patricia, **60,** 85

Prediction: School P.E., **277**

Sleeping and Dreaming, **42**

Steig, William, **114,** 131

Stolz, Mary, **134**

Storm in the Night, **134**

Think Positive!, **210**

Three Little Javelinas, The, **312**

Turnip, The, **280**

What Is Color?, **88**

When I Wake, **174**

Wolf…, A, **172**

Wong, Nellie, **232**

Young, Ed, **288,** 309

Zeny's Zoo, **94**

Acknowledgements

For permission to reprint copyrighted material, grateful acknowledgment is made to the following sources:

Atheneum Books for Young Readers, an imprint of Simon & Schuster: Edited manuscript page from *Me Llamo María Isabel* by Alma Flor Ada. Text copyright © 1993 by Alma Flor Ada. From *My Name Is María Isabel* by Alma Flor Ada, translated from the Spanish by Ana M. Cerro. Text copyright © 1993 by Alma Flor Ada; "The Candles of Hanukkah" copyright © 1990 by Suni Paz (ASCAP).

August House, Inc.: "The Turnip: A Russian Tale" from *Twenty-Two Splendid Tales to Tell from Around the World,* Volume One by Pleasant DeSpain. Text and cover illustration © 1979, 1990, 1994 by Pleasant DeSpain.

Bantam Doubleday Dell Books for Young Readers: Cover illustration by Melodye Rosales from *Jackson Jones and the Puddle of Thorns* by Mary Quattlebaum. Illustration copyright © 1994 by Melodye Rosales.

Children's Better Health Institute, Benjamin Franklin Literary & Medical Society, Inc., Indianapolis, IN: "Kids and Kicks" by Deborah H. Deford from *U. S. Kids, A Weekly Reader Magazine,* October/November 1991. Text copyright © 1991 by Children's Better Health Institute.

Childrens Press, Inc.: From *Sleeping and Dreaming* by Rita Milios. Text copyright © 1987 by Regensteiner Publishing Enterprises, Inc.

Crown Publishers, Inc.: *Lester's Dog* by Karen Hesse, illustrated by Nancy Carpenter. Text copyright © 1993 by Karen Hesse; illustrations copyright (1993 by Nancy Carpenter. Untitled poem (Retitled: "When I Wake . . .") from *Voices of the Wild* by Jonathan London. Text copyright © 1993 by Jonathan London.

Dial Books for Young Readers, a division of Penguin Books USA Inc.: Cover illustration by Jerry Pinkney from *Tanya's Reunion* by Valerie Flournoy. Illustration copyright © 1995 by Jerry Pinkney. Illustrations by Jerry Pinkney from *The Patchwork Quilt* by Valerie Flournoy. Illustrations copyright © 1985 by Jerry Pinkney. Cover illustration by Jerry Pinkney from *John Henry* by Julius Lester. Illustration copyright © 1994 by Jerry Pinkney.

Dutton Children's Books, a division of Penguin Books USA Inc.: *Isla* by Arthur Dorros, illustrated by Elisa Kleven. Text copyright © 1995 by Arthur Dorros; illustrations copyright © 1995 by Elisa Kleven.

Farrar, Straus & Giroux, Inc.: Cover illustration from *Archibald Frisby* by Michael Chesworth. Copyright © 1994 by Michael Chesworth. *Brave Irene* by William Steig. Copyright © 1986 by William Steig.

Naomi F. Faust: "Black Parent to Child" (Retitled: "Parent to Child") from *All Beautiful Things* by Naomi F. Faust. Published by Lotus Press, Detroit, Michigan, distributed by Michigan State University Press.

Hampton-Brown Books: Cover illustration by Raphaelle Goethais from *A Chorus of Cultures* by Alma Flor Ada, Violet J. Harris, and Lee Bennett Hopkins. Copyright © 1993 by Hampton-Brown Books.

Harcourt Brace & Company: "After the Last Hard Freeze" from *In for Winter, Out for Spring* by Arnold Adoff, illustrated by Jerry Pinkney. Text copyright © 1991 by Arnold Adoff; illustrations copyright © 1991 by Jerry Pinkney. Cover photograph from *The Piñata Maker/El Piñatero* by George Ancona. Copyright © 1994 by George Ancona. From *The Science Book of Color* (Retitled: "What Is Color?") by Neil Ardley. Text copyright © 1991 by Neil Ardley. Cover illustration from *The Magic Fan* by Keith Baker. Copyright © 1989 by Keith Baker. Cover illustration by Scott Medlock from *Extra Innings,* selected by Lee Bennett Hopkins. Illustration copyright © 1993 by Scott Medlock. Cover illustration from *Frida María: A Story of the Old Southwest* by Deborah Nourse Lattimore. Copyright © 1994 by Deborah Nourse Lattimore.

HarperCollins Publishers: Cover illustration by Ashley Bryan from *The Story of the Three Kingdoms* by Walter Dean Myers. Illustration copyright © 1995 by Ashley Bryan. *Storm in the Night* by Mary Stolz, illustrated by Pat Cummings. Text copyright © 1988 by Mary Stolz; illustrations copyright © 1988 by Pat Cummings.

Houghton Mifflin Company: Cover illustration by Blair Lent from *The Wave* by Margaret Hodges. Illustration copyright © 1964 by Blair Lent.

Hyperion Books for Children: Illustration by Steve Cieslawski from *At the Crack of the Bat: Baseball Poems,* compiled by Lillian Morrison. Illustration copyright © 1992 by Steve Cieslawski.

Little, Brown and Company: From *Centerfield Ballhawk* by Matt Christopher. Text copyright © 1992 by Matthew F. Christopher. Cover illustration by Peter Parnall from *Annie and the Old One* by Miska Miles. Illustration copyright © 1971 by Peter Parnall.

Lothrop, Lee & Shepard Books, a division of William Morrow & Company, Inc.: Cover illustration by Alan Tiegreen from *Ramona Quimby, Age 8* by Beverly Cleary. Copyright © 1981 by Beverly Cleary.

Macmillan Publishing Company: Cover illustration by Jerry Pinkney from *Turtle in July* by Marilyn Singer. Illustration copyright © 1989 by Jerry Pinkney.

Mike Makley: "The New Kid" by Mike Makley.

Morrow Junior Books, a division of William Morrow & Company, Inc.: Cover illustration by Alan Tiegreen from *Ramona the Brave* by Beverly Cleary. Copyright © 1975 by Beverly Cleary. *City Green* by DyAnne DiSalvo-Ryan. Copyright © 1994 by DyAnne DiSalvo-Ryan.

Northland Publishing, Flagstaff, AZ: *The Three Little Javelinas* by Susan Lowell, illustrated by Jim Harris. Text copyright © 1992 by Susan Lowell; illustrations copyright © 1992 by Jim Harris.

Philomel Books: *Appelemando's Dreams* by Patricia Polacco. Copyright © 1991 by Patricia Polacco. *Lon PoPo: A Red-Riding Hood Story from China* by Ed Young. Copyright © 1989 by Ed Young.

Plays, Inc.: "The Mystery of the Sounds in the Night" by Joan Lowery Nixon from *PLAYS: The Drama Magazine for Young People,* October 1990. Text copyright © 1990 by Plays, Inc. This play is for reading purposes only; for permission to produce, write to Plays, Inc., 120 Boylston Street, Boston, MA 02116.

Marian Reiner, on behlaf of Isabel Joshlin Glaser: "Playing Outfield" by Isabel Joshlin Glaser. Text copyright © 1993 by Isabel Joshlin Glaser. "Prediction: School P. E." by Isabel Joshlin Glaser. Text copyright © 1990 by Isabel Joshlin Glaser.

Rizzoli International Publications, Inc., New York: Cover illustration by Du_an Petricic from *The Color of Things* by Vivienne Shalom. Illustration copyright © 1995 by Du_an Petricic.

Simon & Schuster Books for Young Readers, a division of Simon & Schuster: Cover illustration by Jerry Pinkney from *Half a Moon and One Whole Star* by Crescent Dragonwagon. Illustration copyright © 1986 by Jerry Pinkney. Cover illustration from *Up Goes the Skyscraper!* by Gail Gibbons. Copyright © 1986 by Gail Gibbons. Cover illustration by Floyd Cooper from *Papa Tells Chita a Story* by Elizabeth Fitzgerald Howard. Illustration copyright © 1995 by Floyd Cooper. Cover illustration by Marjorie Priceman from *Zin! Zin! Zin! A Violin* by Lloyd Moss. Illustration copyright © 1995 by Marjorie Priceman. Cover illustration from *Dinosaur Dream* by Dennis Nolan. Copyright © 1990 by Dennis Nolan.

Smithsonian Institution Press, Washington, DC: Untitled poem (Retitled: "A wolf . . .") from *Teton Sioux Music,* translated by Frances Densmore, in Bureau of American Ethnology, Bulletin #61.

Weekly Reader Corporation: "Think Positive!" from *Current Health® 1* Magazine, April 1993. Text copyright © 1993 by Weekly Reader Corporation.

Nellie Wong: "How a Girl Got Her Chinese Name" from *Dreams in Harrison Railroad Park* by Nellie Wong. Published by Kelsey Street Press, 1977.

Wordsong, Boyds Mills Press, Inc.: Cover illustration by John Ward from *Families: Poems Celebrating the African American Experience,* selected by Dorothy S. Strickland and Michael R. Strickland. Illustration copyright © 1994 by John Ward.

Photo Credits

Key: (t) top, (b) bottom, (c) center, (l) left, (r) right, (i) inset, (bg) background.

Jonathan Kim/Gamma Liaison, 2; Joe Devenney/The Image Bank, 3(bg); Maria Taglienti/The Image Bank, 3; Index Stock Photography, 42-43(bg), 44-45(bg); Andy Cox/Tony Stone Images, 44(b/l); David De Lossy/The Image Bank, 44(b/r), 50-51, 51(b/l); Steve Cavalier/Picture Perfect USA, 44-45; Superstock, 45(t), 259(t/r), 260-261(bg), 91(singer); 91(butterfly); Maltaverne/Picture Perfect USA, 45(b); Haraldo de Farla Castro/FPG International, 46(b); Craig Tuttle/The Stock Market, 46-47(bg)t, 50-51(bg); David W. Hamilton/The Image Bank, 46-47; Tom Tracy/Tony Stone Images, 47(t); Roy Gumpel/Gamma Liaison, 47(c); Tom Stewart/The Stock Market, 47(b); Philippe Plailly/Science Photo Library/Photo Researchers, 49; Bryan F. Peterson/The Stock Market, 50(t), 90(baseball); Dennis Berry/Stock Boston, 50(b); The Bettmann Archive, 52, 55; Icon Comm/FPG International, 52-53(bg); Blumebild/FPG International, 53; Grant V. Faint/The Image Bank, 54-55(bg); Blumebild/FPG International, 53; Grant V. Faint/The Image Bank, 54-55(bg); The Bettmann Archive, 55; John Lei/OPC, 60, 90(flashlight/glasses), 91(glasses), 92(paper, pens, scissors), 93(bowls), 98, 100-101, 102, 107, 114, 232-233, 288; Harcourt Brace & Company, 82-83, 103, 258; C. Middlebrook/Picture Perfect USA, 88-89(pencils); Stuart Frawley/Picture Perfect USA, 88(white light); James Randkiev/Tony Stone Images, 88-89(grass); Uniphoto, 88(rose); Stuart Westmorland/Tony Stone Images, 89(fish); P&M Walton/Picture Perfect USA, 89(rainbow); Aitch/Picture Perfect USA, 89(CD); SP Productions/Picture Perfect USA, 90-91(sunset); Otto Rogge/The Stock market, 90-91(geese); B. F. Peterson/WestStock, 91(parrot); Tim Davis/Tony Stone Images, 92(frog); Renee Lynn/Tony Stone Images, 92(leaf); Comstock, 93(paint cans), 93(paint motif); Wally Emerson, 94-95; Courtesy of Jerry Pinkney, 99, 102(t), 106; Antonio Rosario/The Image Bank, 104-105(bg); Chuck Savage/The Stock Market, 104-105(i); (clockwise from top) Charles Thatcher/Tony Stone Images; Gary S. Chapman/The Image Bank; Bruce Ayres/Tony Stone Images; Jay Freis/The Image Bank; Ed Wheeler/The Stock Market; Michael Melford/The Image Bank; Charles Thatcher/Tony Stone Images; Melchior DelGiacomo/The Image Bank; Wenberg-Clark/The Image Bank; Co Rentmeester/The Image Bank; Jon Feinger/The Stock Market; Alan Levenson/Tony Stone Images; David W. Hamilton/The Image Bank; Bruce Ayres/Tony Stone Images; Kay Chernush/The Image Bank; David W. Hamilton/The Image Bank; Walter Bibikow/The Image Bank; Gary Gladstone/The Image Bank, 104-105; Courtesy of Jerry Pickney, 106; Tony Stone Images, 159; Dale Higgins/Harcourt Brace & Company, 230; Sal DiMarco/Black Star/Harcourt Brace & Company, 255; Matt Bradley, 259(t/l), 259(c), 259(b), 260-261; Nancy Pierce/Black Star/Harcourt Brace & Company, 275(l); Courtesy of Matt Christopher, 275(r); Tom Sobolik/Black Star/Harcourt Brace & Company, 309; Ross Humphreys, 328; Davis Photography, 329

Illustration Credits

Guy Porfirio, Cover art

Theme 1: Wayne Vincent, 6-7, 13-17, 108
Theme 2: Doug Bowles, 8-9, 110-113, 236
Theme 3: Jeanne Berg, 10-13, 237, 238-241, 333

Nancy Carpenter, 1-2, 178-209; Leslie Wu, 1,2,6,10,14; Liz Callen, title page, 2,10-11,13,17; Elisa Kleven, 18-39; Richard McNeel, 52-54; Particia Polacco, 60-87; Diane Blasius, 93; Jerry Pinkney, 96-103, 106-107, 284-285; David Flaherty, 99; William Steig, 114-133; Liz Callen, 114-131; Pat Cummings, 134-161; Cameron Wasson, 162-164, 167, 170-171; John Clapp, 172-173; David Diaz, 174-175; Jose Cruz, 212-215; Leslie Wu, 216-231, 234-235; DyAnne DiSalvo-Ryan, 242-257; Obadinah Heavner, 258-261; Steve Cieslawski, 276-277; Lisa Pomerantz, 264-275, 278-279; Holly Cooper, 280-283; Ed Young, 288-311; Jim Harris, 312-331